To: Janet

On our 21st Wedding
Anniversary) May 5, 20__

Love!
Vinku

With This Ring

Mary Motley Kalergis

With This Ring

A PORTRAIT OF MARRIAGE

MARY MOTLEY KALERGIS

The Chrysler Museum of Art
Norfolk, Virginia

Venues: *With This Ring: A Portrait of Marriage*

The Chrysler Museum of Art, Norfolk, Virginia
June 13 through September 7, 1997

Southeast Museum of Photography, Daytona Beach, Florida
October 14, 1997 through January 16, 1998

Rawls Museum Arts, Courtland, Virginia
March 26 through April 25, 1998

Waterworks Visual Arts Center, Salisbury, North Carolina
September 18 through November 15, 1998

Bayly Art Museum of the University of Virginia, Charlottesville, Virginia
June 15 through September 15, 1999

Frontispiece: Vaughn & Pat Kalian, 1993

ISBN: 0-940744-67-8

Library of Congress Catalog Card Number: 97-66096

Design: Germaine Clair

Editor: Terri Denison

Printing: Mondadori A.M.E. Publishing Ltd.

Printed and bound in Italy.

To my husband, David, who can see my work through my eyes.

CONTENTS

FOREWORD

One might say that Mary Kalergis' photography documents human experience. This is not to say, however, that her work is simply documentary; it is far more complex. More than merely recording images and words, her work analyzes and comments. Through choice of projects and subjects, she examines a wide range of human values. These concepts are then composed into a meaningful and coherent statement of universal truth.

Two of her previous books, *Giving Birth* and *Mother: A Collective Portrait,* began with first hand experiences. Although the projects developed from personal interest, she expanded upon the underlying themes to make them interesting to others, precisely as good writers and artists do. Her third book, *Home of the Brave,* also examines the human experience, this time documenting recent immigrants to America. Through her photographs and the words of her subjects, this book is an inspiring exploration of what it means to be an American, and why people from all over the world still seek to join this country of immigrants.

In 1989, The Chrysler Museum of Art collaborated with Mary Kalergis on the Home of the Brave exhibition; organizing and traveling it to three venues. That exhibition met with such success that we are delighted to once again work with Mary Kalergis on her most recent project. By supporting *With This Ring: A Portrait of Marriage,* The Chrysler Museum of Art continues its tradition of publishing, and exhibiting in the Alice and Sol B. Frank gallery, noteworthy photographic work.

With This Ring is not a book about the act of getting married. It is a book that examines why and how people practice the activity of marriage. Among the questions addressed are: Why do people decide to enter into the institution of marriage? How do they grow within a growing relationship? What hardships will be faced and how will they be handled? How do two individuals merge to become a stronger single force? What does a lifetime together mean? This book examines these issues and reveals how each couple, in their own manner, establishes a relationship that functions, or doesn't. This work considers the uniqueness of those relationships.

Although *With This Ring* is not intended to discourage anyone from entering into marriage, it will certainly give pause to those anticipating the nuptial agreement, encouraging them to fathom the implications of the institution, and perhaps, to beware of some of the pitfalls. Yet, this book is not a "how to" guide to marriage — it is one artist's interpretation of it through the people she photographed and the words they spoke.

With This Ring should be perused by every couple considering marriage. It is also a book that everyone who has ever been married will find themselves smiling and thinking "isn't that the truth!"

Brooks Johnson
Curator of Photography
The Chrysler Museum of Art

PREFACE

Like everything which is not the involuntary result of fleeting emotion, but the creation of time
and will, any marriage, happy or unhappy, is infinitely more interesting and significant than any
romance, however passionate.

— W. H. Auden

The institution of marriage is idealized and therefore often criticized. A cynic might say "show me one truly happy married couple," but a reasonable response is "show me one truly happy single person." Neither responsibility nor freedom guarantee "happily ever after," but marriage does more than provide shelter for our young or tax advantages. At its best it creates a safe haven where, with the gift of time given by the ideal of lifelong commitment, people can fully reveal themselves and reach ever-deepening bonds of intimacy. No longer just individuals, they become part of something stronger — a couple, a family, and a community.

Idealism can turn to bitterness if we aren't sympathetic to the foibles of our mates. We are taught that to err is human, but to forgive, divine. Empathy is the key to forgiveness and this forgiveness is the secret of an enduring marriage, where love not only survives, but thrives.

Of course not every marriage lasts a lifetime, but whatever your formal religion or lack thereof, viewing marriage as something bigger than two people living together helps it grow stronger through the years. Many of the couples in this book who had weathered the inevitable hardships of life said, "we formed our own religion." By thinking less about what they wanted at the moment, and more about whom they wanted to be over a lifetime, they were able to grow together instead of apart.

The honesty with which people face the camera and talk about such personal subjects continually amazes me. Revealing themselves "on the record," the people in these pages are subject to misunderstanding and judgement, but they teach us that the institution of marriage embodies more than just slogans or stereotypes. It is ancient but alive, embodied in the personal experiences of real people, and through their generosity, we can explore the mystery of our ideals.

INTRODUCTION

When Mary Kalergis asked if I might say a few words about this project, it seemed an exciting possibility. In the back of my mind, though, I wondered what could be added to the viewer's understanding of, or automatic interest in, images of couples that already seem quite dynamic and involving. Though I'm primarily a writer of fiction, I'm sure I'm so drawn to photography because my sense of a story is, in its inception, so rooted in the visual; it's much more of an impetus than plot, or, in the beginning, even character. If a photograph involves, or relies on symbolism, it is easy for a literary person to describe. But Kalergis is not a symbolist. She is not intrusive about orchestrating contexts — or in seizing the inherent contradictions and telling details that might go far in defining her subject. She is also light of touch, not heavy-handed in setting people up so that the image they present says one thing, while their environment mitigates or otherwise tempers their expression of themselves. The way she has posed her subjects is uncontrived, but not uninformative. It's interesting to look at the poses people seem to have fallen into: couples who lean toward one another, as if drawn by magnetic force; the self-aware, slightly self-parodic pose that remains a good joke, even after we've all discovered it early on in life; or the photograph that features another photograph within it, with perhaps one more photograph, even smaller.

In considering the group photographs, I was struck by how much everyone occupies their own space. (Consider the family portrait of the Portnoys, and also the dual portrait of Ludwig and Beatrice Kuttner.) In other photographs, we see a movement from darkness to light (Bob and Julie Gottschalk), in which a moment of joint repose still offers a glimpse of personal separateness. A kind of movement within stillness is created by the shift from dark to light: her dark hair and coat; his pale hair and jacket — and this is echoed by the background, which in moving from dark to light, seems to reinforce the couple's dark/light polarity. Similarly, but with a much different dynamic, Martin Rubenstein and Martin Schwartz, appear united by darkness, but spotlit as if a beam of something in the future is drawing them: their attention is undivided.

For most of the photographs, Kalergis has come in close: couples are posed in a doorway; they sit and stand in the foreground of almost obliterated backgrounds; faces often crowd the lens. This is risky, for obvious reasons: if we can't imaginatively make ourselves part of their world — if we are left only with people we do not know — those people must be recognizable, yet surprising, reminiscent of the familiar, yet at the same time unfamiliar, unusual enough to involve us. When a photograph is made of a couple or a family within an enclosed space, and when the photographer seems not to be distant, but almost an invisible member of the group due to sheer proximity, it seems to me that the photograph has the burden of asking to be perceived as somehow definitive — that the viewer is asked to omit the world (never easily done) and to trust instead this new, narrow, restricted world. As part of the photographic process, the photographer has the task not only of becoming personally familiar with what she sees, but of wearing down, waiting out, or otherwise biding time until the right moment comes to make the photograph. At the same time, the photographer must be open to surprise and to happenstance, if she is to present people she knows (at least, better than we do), but whom, through her photograph, she may also come to know better.

I'm sure we've all seen photographs in which we suspect that the subject is responding — perhaps primarily to the photographer. Consider some of the faces in Avedon's *In the American West,* and it is difficult to imagine that the photographer was not a strong presence. It was Diane Arbus' particular talent to appear to absent herself from a close-up photograph — to vaporize only a few inches from the faces she was photographing. For an obvious symbiosis between photographer and subject, consider the late Tom Victor's photographs of dancers performing, or his portraits of writers. Look at Rollie McKenna's photographs of James Merrill or of Elizabeth Bishop. Or Bob Adelman's portraits taken during the civil rights movement and, later, his photographs of his friend Raymond Carver. Adelman's book is called simply, *Carver Country.* It seems to me, if I can make a metaphoric claim, that we all have countries: places that define us; ourselves, in turn, defining places.

In Kalergis' photographs, she is after something different, though she is clearly interested in the American terrain. While the subjects in this book are diverse, the photographer believes in simple domesticity as a uniting, defining force; she is interested in people who stand, largely, separate from their environment, but rooted in whatever environment they have created (the photographs on park benches, or out on a lawn with surfboards, are a rare departure). And always, their faces, their bodies, are allowed to speak for themselves. Avedon's white drop-sheet would be too artificial — but what about Kalergis' somewhat similar method in zeroing in enough so that the outside is opaque, or for all intents and purposes gone? What about providing only the existing, rather than an expedient telling detail (curtains and blurry backgrounds tell us little)?

If you think that coming close to people — especially with a camera — is likely to produce anything but fear, self-consciousness, and strangeness, you've been standing at a great distance (as we tend to) with your Instamatic. What Mary Kalergis does must speak of a faith that what we are will come through regardless of context; that if God is to be found in the details, those details should not be neglected just because they are quite ordinary. These photographs are a testament to the ordinary, the power of the everyday. To the inherent mystery of how people live and embrace. To the unknowableness of life behind closed doors, yet the titillation of spying because someone seems to have permeated these walls.

Photographs are a record, but at their best they are also a revelation. When a picture is made, it may be prized for one thing, but years later — when Spot the dog is dead, and Dad's ponytail is long gone — photographs are a nugget of nostalgia, having different associations, different connotations than when they were first taken. If they're wrong, they're vulnerable to change in a way that makes them dismissable. If they're right, it is probably because they always had particular power, an energy that transcended time, a conviction about them that, while still difficult to describe, nevertheless remains impossible to paraphrase.

What will this book look like in 20 or 30 years? It will look like life in America. It will look, I suspect, as if a non-intrusive photographer took unorchestrated pictures, dwelling on her subjects at the same time she allowed them freedom. It might be the liner notes you study years after having listened to the music again and again, learning what inspired the song you already love, appreciating the anecdote that's sure to make you smile when next you hear that particular guitar break.

Ann Beattie

CHAPTER 1

"We can question everything except our commitment to each other. That is our sacred oath."

LINDLEY & YUKARI FRAHM

LINDLEY MET YUKARI IN CALIFORNIA JUST AS SHE WAS FINISHING A TOUR OF THE UNITED STATES. THEY WERE TOGETHER ONLY THREE DAYS BEFORE SHE HAD TO RETURN HOME TO JAPAN. AFTER TELEPHONE CALLS AND CORRESPONDENCE, LINDLEY FOLLOWED HER. WITHIN A WEEK OF HIS ARRIVAL, THEY WERE ENGAGED. YUKARI SAYS HER MOTHER ENCOURAGED HER TO FOLLOW HER HEART. HER MOTHER HAD FOLLOWED THE WISHES OF HER OWN PARENTS AND MADE AN UNHAPPY MARRIAGE. SHE KNEW THE RISK OF PLAYING IT SAFE. LOSING YUKARI TO A FOREIGN CULTURE WAS BETTER THEN PRESSURING HER TO GIVE UP HER CHANCE FOR A GOOD MARRIAGE.

Lindley: She lived in another country and I didn't want to live without her once I met her. Marriage is a declarative act, a public acknowledgement of a private commitment. It is a framework for us to live our life. After you have children together, your commitment to each other is even bigger than yourselves. It's not just what you want anymore, your decisions are based on what is right for the entire family. If marriage is a trap, we set the trap ourselves.

Yukari: I certainly didn't come to America to find a husband. I was curious about the United States and attracted to its optimism, but until I met Lindley, I didn't think I'd ever come back to visit.

Lindley: I had never met an American girl who was so candid and trustworthy.

Yukari: I can talk to Lindley about anything and he treats me with respect. More than that, when I'm discouraged he says, "Your words create. If you can think it, you can make it happen." He pushes me forward and holds me up and encourages me to become all I can be. His willingness to support me makes me want to support him in return.

Lindley: It is the opposite of competition, which I'd often experienced in previous relationships. I am in the driver's seat about financial decisions, but I'll always concede to Yukari on issues about raising our boys. Concede might be too strong a word. Actually, she often changes my mind through her point of view. She has also changed my mind about certain career strategies.

Yukari: A Japanese man would often expect his wife to demure to his decision.

Lindley: She's so much smarter, I would be crazy not to consider her opinion.

Yukari: Our problems have been frustrations over Lindley's career, not really our relationship. The best gift we can give our children, much more important than Lindley's income, is a good relationship, a happy family.

"If marriage is a trap, we set the trap ourselves."

RODNEY & TAMMY HARDING

FOR YOUNG-MARRIEDS TAMMY AND RODNEY HARDING, THE PRESCRIPTION FOR A GOOD MARRIAGE IS AS SIMPLE AS SPENDING TIME TOGETHER, WORKING TO HAVE A PLACE OF THEIR OWN, AND FINDING A WAY TO HANDLE THEIR DISPUTES — THEY "DON'T GO TO BED MAD."

Rodney: We straighten things out pretty quickly.

Tammy: We don't go to bed mad, and in the morning our disagreement is gone.

Rodney: I finally got a pretty good job in construction and we're sorting out our future.

Tammy: Our number one goal is to own our own home.

Rodney: And a kid on down the line. One, maybe two.

Tammy: Not a lot — too many headaches.

Rodney: I've lost touch with most of my single friends now that I'm married. Tammy and I like to go shopping or to the movies when we're not working. On the weekends we might visit our families.

Tammy: We do the cooking together, we go to the laundromat together. We kinda stick to ourselves.

Rodney: Now that we are both working, seems like things have evened out. When the construction jobs were slow, I felt bad that Tammy had to pull more than her share.

Tammy: You were a lot harder on yourself about it than I was. It's hard starting out on your own, but I always believed we would make it.

Rodney: But I am pretty easy to get along with. If she wants to do something, I'll back her up. Neither one of us wants to be the boss. I was around that growing up and it doesn't work. I don't want to control her and I don't want her to control me. If she disagrees with me, I'll listen and if I think it's a good disagreement, I'll change my mind.

Tammy: Rodney always has to ask what's bothering me when he sees me get quiet; but he'll always speak right out as soon as he has something to say. I like it that he cares. He won't let me hide from him or myself.

"We straighten things out pretty quickly."

"He won't let me hide from him or myself."

BILL CAMPBELL & MARYANNE VOLLERS

BILL CAMPBELL AND MARYANNE VOLLERS HAD HIGH-PACED, DEMANDING CAREERS BEFORE MARRYING (BOTH FOR THE FIRST TIME). BILL WAS A PHOTOJOURNALIST FOR *Time* MAGAZINE, BASED OUT OF AFRICA, AND MARYANNE WAS AN EDITOR WITH *Rolling Stone* MAGAZINE IN NEW YORK. THEY MET WHEN MARYANNE WAS VISITING NAIROBI. SHE STAYED FOR SIX YEARS, WORKING WITH BILL TO COVER WARS, REVOLUTIONS, FAMINES, AND THE VANISHING AFRICAN WILDLIFE. THE YEAR BEFORE THIS PORTRAIT AND INTERVIEW, THEY HAD RETURNED TO THE UNITED STATES AND BEGUN BUILDING THEIR "DREAM HOUSE" IN THE VIRGINIA COUNTRYSIDE.

Bill: When we first met, I was drinking too much and sick with malaria a lot. I was going from one war to the next revolution.

Maryanne: There was no place for a woman in that life.

Bill: That used to worry me. I had a big defense built up where I wouldn't let myself get too close to anybody, because if I did, I wouldn't want to travel and then I would lose my job, which at that time in my life was my whole identity.

Maryanne: It was touch and go for a while. I would back off when I would see him struggle. Come to think of it, this instinct probably allowed us to stay together. Eventually though, I said I was either working and traveling with him or I was going in the opposite direction. I wasn't going to stay behind and wait for him.

Bill: It seemed like the best idea was to get two round-the-world tickets and stay together, and that was it. Being on the road together, working side by side, made us even closer. My favorite subject in the whole world is rhinos, and she wrote the best rhino story I had ever read. She could get along with all these heavy duty macho guys. I'll never forget the day she sighted a rhino in an automatic rifle on the Zimbabwe River. We've been to some really awful places, both together and on our own — so we can really share our experiences.

Maryanne: (laughing) If you want to marry an Eagle Scout, you had better learn how to track.

Bill: That helps.

Maryanne: Actually, we are very much alike.

Bill: We are equally sloppy and always looking for an excuse to drink champagne.

Maryanne: Adapting to Bill is almost like rediscovering myself. I grew up in the country, but over the years became a prisoner of rock-and-roll, a city girl riding around in a limousine. I took a chance to change my life, and went to Africa. I knew it was going to be an adventure and, sure enough, I met Bill and it has been quite an adventure, a hell of a ride!

*"We are both
equally sloppy
and always
looking for an
excuse to drink
champagne."*

KURT & TAMARA TOTTEN

KURT AND TAMARA CONSIDER MARRIAGE A SACRAMENT.

Tamara: When he graduated from college, we both agreed we would date other people after he left town.

Kurt: She jumped into another relationship right away and I missed her terribly. She had gotten me going to church, and after we were separated I became very involved in Christian studies and was born again.

Tamara: When he told me what had happened to him, I realized that the true faith of my childhood was missing from my life and that was the empty space I felt inside me. I clung so desperately in relationships with men because of this emptiness.

Kurt: We decided to give ourselves a chance again, but as true friends instead of needy lovers. I had to get to know and trust her again. I had to have my pride cut out from under me to make the relationship work. To give yourself up to somebody has nothing to do with pride.

Tamara: We were celibate until we got married two years later. We needed that space to get to know ourselves and God.

Kurt: On our wedding day we were ready to turn over our commitment to celibacy to our commitment to marriage.

Tamara: We wanted our lives to experience a change on our wedding day. Marriage for us is not just a piece of paper.

Kurt: Our wedding rings are symbolic of our total commitment to sharing our lives. We can question everything except our commitment to each other. That is our sacred oath.

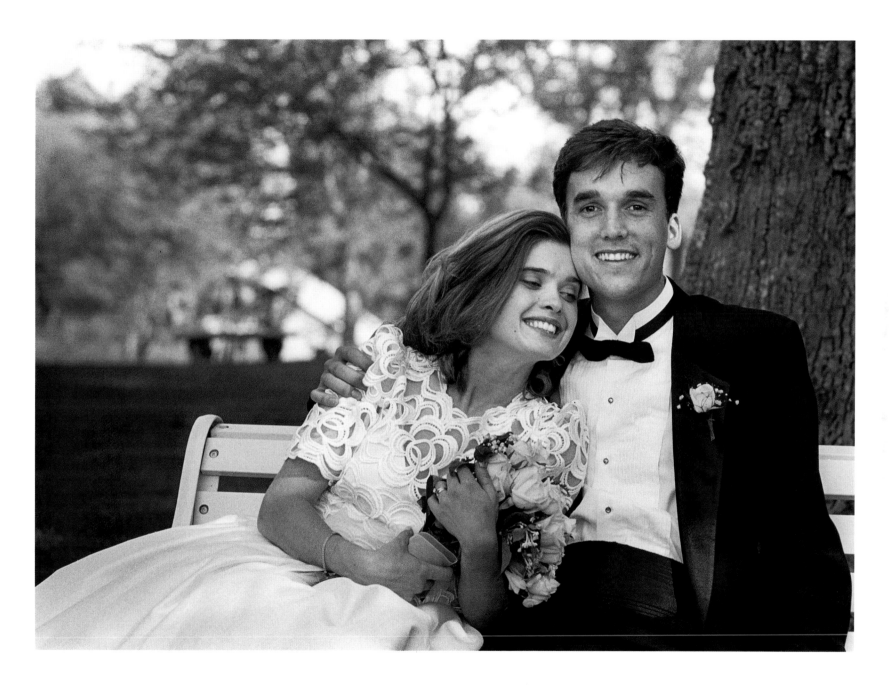

"We can question everything except our commitment to each other. That is our sacred oath."

KIP & LENI SORENSON

KIP AND LENI MET WHEN HE ANSWERED HER "PERSONALS" ADVERTISEMENT IN *MOTHER EARTH NEWS* IN 1973. THEY LIVED TOGETHER FOR 15 YEARS BEFORE MARRYING.

Kip: After my father died, I started thinking about my responsibility to Leni and our kids. In memory of my father, we got married on what would have been his birthday. I was his only son and felt the responsibility to carry on his name. For years, I always felt marriage ruined a perfectly good relationship. I somehow ended up married to a prostitute from Las Vegas while I was still married to my first wife. My history as a husband was not too successful. It took me many years to straighten things out. I was divorced from both of my wives when I answered Leni's letter in Mother Earth *and had no thoughts of marriage when we first met, although there was definitely an immediate attraction there. After 15 years, I started to realize that our relationship was working.*

Leni: Every five years, we'd say, "let's give it another five years." I had been through two disastrous marriages and I did not want to keep repeating myself. Kip's father's death made us less fearful, ready to give it a try.

Kip: I always got a certain satisfaction about tweaking tradition all those years.

Leni: Cohabitation laws define our relationship as "lewd and lascivious," which sounds rather exciting. My father is black and my mother is white. They got married illegally when miscegenation laws were still on the books in California. They lived together for 57 years. That's quite an admirable accomplishment.

Kip: You can't stay together if every day has to be negotiated. Couples who make it through thick and thin are those who accept certain roles and responsibilities and stick by them.

Leni: We watched Kip's parents enjoy their time together after the kids were grown. For 51 years they had plenty to say to each other. That is what we want for the future. It makes growing old seem less intimidating somehow.

*"Every five years we would say,
'Let's give it another five years.'"*

Sat Bir & Siri Krishna Khalsa

Siri Krishna and Sat Bir follow the Sikh religion and look to their spiritual leader, Yogi Bhajan, for guidance in settling important questions. Their marriage was arranged by him before the couple ever met.

Siri Krishna: Marrying in the heat of passion, like I did in my first marriage, gives you rose colored glasses that eventually fade. You are sometimes left with someone you don't have much in common with after the thrill dies down.

Sat Bir: You can't think when you are in lust. The power of the arranged marriage is you get to look at the goals and lifestyle choices while your brain isn't impaired with a flood of hormones. Sikhs don't have sexual union outside of marriage because it can only cloud your judgment on all the other issues.

Siri Krishna: We believe that when you are physically inside of another person, you actually take on the karma of your partner, who becomes part of your vibration for the rest of your life. There is nothing casual about it.

Sat Bir: Sex is a big deal. It is sacrilegious to trivialize it. The sexual act is a spiritual as well as physical union.

Siri Krishna: Yogi Bhajan rarely arranges marriages anymore because people tend to blame him if things don't work out. I knew if I chose to go through with this arranged betrothal that I would be responsible for the outcome. Sat Bir flew me to Virginia over Valentine's Day. We look back on that weekend and call it the Valentine's Day massacre. My faith was being tested almost beyond endurance. I felt no initial attraction to him and I realized I literally had to die, surrender to the process, in order to be reborn....

Sat Bir: ...and understand why the test was there in the first place.

Siri Krishna: Our wedding ceremony is very deep spiritually and it went through us completely. When it was over, we looked at each other and realized the vibration had changed.

Sat Bir: Her whole aura had turned 180 degrees around. There was a whole new person standing in front of me. The struggle was gone and she was totally there. Our courtship had never been a romance, by any stretch of the imagination. But, after the marriage ceremony, I really felt like we were mates. Our drive back to Virginia from New Mexico was really romantic — just like the songs on the radio.

"*Sex is a big deal. It is sacrilegious to trivialize it. The sexual act is a spiritual as well as a physical union.*"

JAMES & ANDREA RIDDLE

JAMES AND ANDREA WERE MARRIED SIX MONTHS BEFORE THIS PORTRAIT AND INTERVIEW WERE MADE, SHORTLY AFTER HER HIGH SCHOOL GRADUATION.

Andrea: Right now is our time to get to spend time together. I would like to be married for at least a year before I get pregnant. I was never allowed to have kids over to play when I was growing up because my mom was super clean and didn't want a mess. Now I have my own place and can do what I want to do.

James: There were six of us in a small place growing up. We didn't have a whole lot of room to have friends over. I like having my own place and room to have friends over. I feel very strongly that I am only going to get married one time. I would be right proud to be married 50 years.

Andrea: I don't plan on ever getting divorced. It happened in my family and it was bad. I would never put my kids through what I have been through, never. Getting married gives me a chance to have a whole family. I was real young when my parents divorced and you never get over feeling alone. I was Daddy's girl, but because I was only six, I had to stay with my mom. Divorce gives you the most lonely feeling. I think as far as divorce and children go, people need to be wiser. Speaking from experience, it can really hurt the children.

James: I like coming home from work and having someone there waiting for me. I don't have to go out looking for someone, because I've already found her.

Andrea: I like the responsibility. Most of all, I really appreciate never having to be alone.

*"I would be
right proud
to be married
50 years."*

Ralph & Mary Moroney

Mary had been married four times previously and widowed twice when she met an Irish bachelor named Ralph Moroney. At the time of this portrait and interview, they had been married a year and a half and Mary was seven months pregnant with their first child. She has three other children.

Mary: *I have made marriage my career! As a little girl, I fantasized about being a bride. Jane Wyatt, Donna Reed, and June Cleaver were my role models.*

Ralph: I don't think I thought about growing up very much when I was a boy. The Irish don't marry until late in life. Maybe because when we do, it's for good. This is my first and last marriage.

Mary: *(laughing) This is my fifth! Someone gave Ralph a hat with a "V" on it. We call him Ralph the Fifth! My problem was I couldn't justify having sex outside of marriage, and it never occurred to me not to have sex! I have two dead husbands, so I felt both cheated and entitled in a lot of ways. In hindsight, I was sometimes reckless and impulsive.*

Ralph: There was always some man hanging around Mary, and I found myself always taking her side. I have a good relationship with her children, and that bound us together.

Mary: *I'm not beating myself up about mistakes I made in the past because they paved the way for me to change and have a relationship with Ralph.*

Ralph: Growing up in Catholic Ireland, I was more than a little bit nervous about getting involved with someone who had been married four times. It was real scary. It had always been Mary's way to build a relationship in bed rather than out. We had a good friendship going and I didn't want to ruin it. You can't build (looks to Mary)....

Mary: *...a house on shifting sand.*

Ralph: It doesn't work. You have to have some sort of decent foundation there. Our friendship meant a great deal to each of us and I was very protective of it.

Mary: *My children were really threatened when I told them Ralph and I were getting married. I was kind of the black widow. Everyone I had fallen in love with either died or went away. They really like him a lot and it was a scary thing for them.*

Ralph: I have to break the curse.

"I was kind of the black widow. Everyone that I had fallen in love with either died or went away."

MERT & JUDY MARTIN

MERT IS A CABINETMAKER AND JUDY A BUSINESS EXECUTIVE. THEY WERE BOTH DIVORCED WITH GROWN CHILDREN WHEN THEY MET AND MARRIED, THREE YEARS BEFORE THIS PORTRAIT WAS TAKEN.

Judy: My job was so pressured and hectic that I came to visit my sister to unwind and be around people who knew how to relax. Mert was building her house. In the first ten minutes we met, I told him the most intimate part of my life, and he told me about his troubles in the past. I informed him I had a daughter who was schizophrenic and he told me he had been an alcoholic.

Mert: I was really taken with her. I had watched her out of the corner of my eye while I was working. We both felt free to talk about everything together. We could identify with each others' struggle. I was shocked to have strong feelings again.

Judy: Since my divorce, five years earlier, I had lived totally in my work and my children. I was addicted to work to block my pain in the same way Mert used alcohol to block his. It was a little frightening to feel love again.

Mert: I decided to go to California to be near her and build a new life for myself and, hopefully, for us.

Judy: Mert calmed me. I undoubtedly believed he was good for me. It was wonderful to feel instead of think. Falling in love awakened a whole new world of emotion for me. It was as if our tuning forks were in perfect harmony.

Mert: Judy has helped me let go of regrets about the past and go on living again, healed and whole.

Judy: Living with Mert has introduced me to a spiritual life that has been very healing for me. He taught me to live my life aspiring to principles greater than myself. Being loved makes me take better care of myself, treat myself with more respect.

"It was a little frightening to feel love again."

MATTHEW & AMY PAPPERT

MATTHEW IS A PSYCHIATRIST AND HOSPITAL ADMINISTRATOR. AMY HAD JUST FINISHED HER INTERNSHIP IN DERMATOLOGY WHEN THIS PORTRAIT AND INTERVIEW WERE MADE. THEY WANT TO HAVE CHILDREN, BUT ARE UNSURE WHEN.

Matthew: How do you ever get to that place where you know you are ready to have kids? I mean, I know theoretically we want to have children one day; but when do you feel like "today is the day?"

Amy: I have dreams about having a baby and then forgetting it's in the bottom drawer of the dresser.

Matthew: I don't have any fantasy about having a wife that devotes all of her time to me. It seems draining in a strange way. I don't want someone drawing an identity off of me.

Amy: His ability to listen saved me during my internship. I want to have a life outside of the hospital. Time to be a wife and mother. One of dermatology's attractions to me is the reasonable hours.

Matthew: After her internship, I feel like we deserve some time together before we start a family.

Amy: The pitter-patter of little feet is definitely not in the near future! My childhood was not easy because my mom was ill for as long as I can remember. Just getting married is a big leap for me. I'm not quite at the point where I feel ready to become a mother. I certainly don't imagine the two of us staying here where we are forever.

Matthew: I believe that cultural institutions like marriage spring from biological needs. We are a species that can't take care of ourselves for many years. Someone needs to take care of the mother while she takes care of the infant, if the species is going to survive. The legalities of the institution spring from these biological necessities.

"*I believe that cultural institutions like marriage spring from biological needs.... Someone needs to take care of the mother while she takes care of the infant if the species is going to survive.*"

CHAPTER 2

"We didn't get married to consciously learn these things."

PAUL & ROSEMARY SUMMERS

PAUL AND ROSEMARY HAD THEIR FIRST CHILD IN THEIR FIRST YEAR OF MARRIAGE.

Rosemary: During the whole pregnancy, I felt that he just didn't understand what I was going through.

Paul: It is hard not to feel left out to a certain extent. Pregnancy puts the husband on the sidelines. Now that she's born, I understand the phrase, "labor of love."

Rosemary: Even though he can participate in her care now that she's here, I still look at him bleary-eyed and realize how much more my life has changed than his. His day is still basically the same. Every waking moment has been different for me since her birth. The first few months I couldn't help but feel anger. It didn't somehow seem fair. If he was five minutes late from work, I'd fall apart. I felt like my whole day was waiting for him to come home and give me some relief.

Paul: I have a different perception towards my own mother now...just realizing she went through all of this with me.

Rosemary: When he gets home from work, he wants to spend time with the baby, but that is the last thing I want to do. I need a break! The poor guy gets home from work and I'm in my room crying while the baby's in her room crying.

Paul: The sleeping habits of a newborn can play hell on your sex life because you are both so tired and overwhelmed with new responsibility. It can be frightening when things change, but then you come to realize that everyone who becomes parents goes through that adjustment and it's just a phase. It's stressful — everything's new.

Rosemary: We can spend hours in bed talking about her diaper rash!

Paul: Changing a dirty diaper right before you get in bed can ruin the mood for romance.

Rosemary: When we went out to dinner on our first anniversary, all we could talk about was the baby.

Paul: Sometimes we laugh and wonder what we *did* talk about before she was born!

"...I still look at him bleary-eyed and realize how much more my life has changed than his."

DAVID & NEILA SMITH

DAVID AND NEILA MET IN INDIA, WHERE SHE WAS A PHYSICIAN AND HE WAS A MEMBER OF THE UNITED STATES FOREIGN SERVICE. ALTHOUGH BOTH WERE PREVIOUSLY MARRIED (HE WAS DIVORCED AND SHE WAS WIDOWED) THEY FIND THAT NOTHING COULD HAVE COMPLETELY PREPARED THEM FOR THE CHALLENGES OF STARTING A NEW LIFE TOGETHER IN AMERICA.

Neila: When two fully formed adults join together, there are a lot of adjustments. Everything from when and what we eat, to our relationships with our grown children is something to be worked out. David calls it a growing process, I call it getting bent-out-of-shape! The absence of my family and friends affected me more deeply than I anticipated, so our first year of marriage has been anything but smooth sailing.

David: Neila has a very low threshold for tears and that's something I've had to adjust to. I can't run away from her feelings or mine. She just expresses hers differently. Most problems are resolvable if the commitment to resolve them is there. Loving someone leaves you so vulnerable and exposed that it's impossible not to hurt each other from time to time.

Neila: We are both very verbal people, but couples often negotiate and communicate without a word exchanged between them.

David: Maybe in America, even more than older cultures and traditions, we acknowledge, even encourage, the fact that people change. This almost certainly leads to higher divorces, if the change is not compatible. It's the price you pay for the freedom to grow and express yourself. My definition of life is change. The idea of a marriage where the partners are stuck in certain roles is deadening to me.

Neila: Just because you negotiate terms today doesn't mean those terms will work for you in a few years.

David: If you acknowledge that life is change, then your marriage should outlast the difficult stretches, because just like the fun part, everything is subject to change. What we are struggling with right now is how to live our lives now that our dreams have come true. For so long, our struggle was getting together. Now it is staying together.

"What we are struggling with is how to live our lives now that our dreams have come true."

GARY & CANDI VESSEL

GARY AND CANDI HAVE OVERCOME DISAPPROVING PARENTS AND THE USUAL CHALLENGES OF YOUNG MARRIED LIFE TO CREATE SOMETHING THAT IS UNIQUELY THEIR OWN, AND YET, SOMEHOW VERY FAMILIAR IN ITS DESCRIPTION.

Gary: She's had to go through a lot more changes since our marriage than I have. My mom was kind of hard on her.

Candi: I remember her looking right at me and saying to Gary, "Love is blind."

Gary: We're totally on each other's side. There's no need for secrets.

Candi: It is like Gary and I have forged our own religion. He's my best friend. We figure things out as we go along. I don't have to protect him from anything. We are both right out there for each other.

Gary: Married life suits me fine — I've always been a homebody. Even as a little kid, I didn't like to go out much. I know the job that I do outside of the house is not nearly as emotionally and physically demanding as staying home all day with small children.

Candi: It is no sacrifice for me. It's something I want to do. I feel kind of guilty that I've given up practicing [the viola]. I just lost my focus since I got pregnant. There for a while, I got in to a baking binge.

Gary: One day I came home to five desserts!

Candi: Having kids has changed me more than marriage.

Gary: I'm doing exactly what I want to be doing. We might not have a lot of money, but I like my work and love my wife and child. I hope I can learn from my mom's mistakes and be more supportive of my own children.

"It's like Gary and I have forged our own religion."

Ronald & Zarina (Ann) Gordon

ANN CAME FROM NAIROBI, KENYA, TO BE A HOME CARE ATTENDANT FOR RON, WHO DEPENDS UPON A WHEELCHAIR FOR HIS PHYSICAL MOBILITY. THEIR MUTUAL ATTRACTION WAS IMMEDIATE.

Ron: *We seemed like family almost immediately.*

Ann: Our relationship was so comfortable, so immediately established that it seemed like a continuation of something that existed in the past.

Ron: *There is a real sense of destiny and fate in our union. We have both been married before, but our previous marriages were much narrower, our roles as husband and wife were more fixed. Ann and I operate on many different levels; father and daughter, mother and son, husband and wife, as well as friends and lovers. Even though I am 16 years older, she is just as likely to mother me as I am to be a father figure to her. Although she gives me nursing care, I never think of her as my nurse.*

Ann: We can act like children together. When you trust each other and feel understood, it can make you feel playful.

Ron: *There is a fragility in the relationship that can't withstand the stresses of life if you get too stuck in a singular role. If you are always the strong one or the passive one, the cheerful one — whatever — it eventually paints you into a corner that you won't be able to get out of.*

Ann: When you get married as a mature adult, you have a clearer sense of your own values and can therefore express yourself more clearly than when you were young.

Ron: *The beauty and strength in the fluidity of roles that I mentioned earlier is you don't have to filter your thoughts and feelings from your mate. You can say what you're thinking at that moment and your partner won't be disappointed because you didn't live up to some established expectation.*

"When you get married as a mature adult, you have a clearer sense of your own values and can therefore express yourself more clearly than when you were young."

JOHN & DIANE LEGGE

BOTH JOHN'S AND DIANE'S FIRST MARRIAGES WERE DESTROYED BY THEIR ALCOHOLISM. THEY MET AT AN ALCOHOLICS ANONYMOUS MEETING. AT THE TIME OF THEIR PORTRAIT AND INTERVIEW, THEY HAD BEEN MARRIED FOR THREE YEARS.

John: If we had met when we were still drinking, we would never have gotten along.

Diane: He was a redneck and I was a flower child! When we first met, I'd been sober for five years and Johnny had only been in the program for six months. I remember saying to myself, "I'm not touching him with a ten foot pole" because it takes at least a year or more to acclimate to sobriety and learn a new way of being. Four dates later we started living together. That was six years ago. The 12 step AA program is a strong common bond between us, yet at the same time we don't over-analyze things.

John: She was so supportive of my struggle to stay sober in the early years. It's hard to imagine that she could have been so understanding if she hadn't fought the same battle. I used to go to AA meetings six or seven times a week. Over the years, our own life together has replaced the fellowship of AA and we just go to meetings occasionally.

Diane: I think it would be harder to be the mate of an alcoholic, than the alcoholic when he first joins AA because, at the beginning, it's a very self-centered program. All your energy is spent saving yourself. Unless you've experienced the black hole of alcoholism, I don't know if you can understand it. The hardest thing we had to get through was my problem with his son from the first marriage. It was hard for me to be a stepmother — I was jealous of the bond between them and wasn't used to being around little kids. It took me about four years to work it out.

John: At first she couldn't understand how much I missed him.

Diane: In hindsight it seems really selfish, but never having or even wanting a child myself, I couldn't understand that connection. It used to hurt my feelings that he'd be depressed about being away from his son instead of being delighted to be with me.

John: Things started turning around when I realized I had to stop trying to make Diane and my boy get along. I had to step back and let them work it out for themselves.

Diane: I adore that kid now, we really feel like a family when we are together. I think the hardest thing for a couple to figure out is how to be supportive without trying to solve each other's problems.

"*I think that the hardest thing for a couple to figure out is how to be supportive without trying to solve each other's problems.*"

Barclay & Aggie Rives

MARRIED THREE YEARS WHEN THIS PORTRAIT AND INTERVIEW WERE MADE, BARCLAY AND AGGIE ARE PICTURED WITH THEIR TWO-YEAR-OLD DAUGHTER, CAROLINE.

Barclay: We don't make a lot of arbitrary demands on each other. We both have a tremendous amount of independence and we encourage each other's creativity.

Aggie: We are on the same team. It's not always easy to live with someone. Think about how hard it was sometimes with your own family growing up; yet it's hard to live alone. I never liked it.

Barclay: I lived alone for nine years, and in general I like it; yet the loneliness was sometimes very troublesome. Occasional friction is a small price to pay to share your life with someone you love.

Aggie: I find the friction in our relationship is often that I project my anger at myself onto my husband. Our conflicts are from a clash of values because, obviously, we were raised as children in two different households and every family has its unique assumptions.

Barclay: I think Aggie is right. If I am able to step back and examine why something she has done is irritating me, it's usually because it's something I'm struggling against myself.

Aggie: I think one of the most interesting things about marriage is that it creates an opportunity for you to mirror each other and learn a lot about yourself.

Barclay: I know myself a lot better from sharing these past years with Aggie.

Aggie: We didn't get married to consciously learn these things. Lessons unfold over time. It is a constant discovery.

"We didn't get married to
consciously learn these things."

BOB & JULIE GOTTSCHALK

BOB, AN INTERNATIONAL LAWYER, MET JULIE IN A MUSEUM IN PARIS WHEN SHE WAS WORKING AS AN AU PAIR. THIRTY-TWO YEARS HER SENIOR, HE AVIDLY PURSUED HER UNTIL SHE SAID "YES." AT THE TIME THIS PORTRAIT AND INTERVIEW WERE MADE, THEY HAD BEEN MARRIED TEN YEARS AND HAD TWO SONS.

Julie: Our first conversation was one I'll never forget. I had the feeling I had known him always. There was definitely something powerful happening, but I didn't interpret it as love.

Bob: I chased her through Paris, Miami, California — flying almost every weekend on the red eye special.

Julie: He drove me crazy....

Bob: Eventually she joined me in New York.

Julie: I couldn't figure out how to say "no." I was intimidated by his power and persistence, not his age — he was married three times before me, which was pretty hard to explain to my friends and family.

Bob: I just wanted to be with her at all costs. I wasn't very concerned about what my friends thought; though I know my fanatic courtship caused them some concern. All I could think of was that I didn't want to lose her.

Julie: I was so young when we got married, I didn't have any specific goals, except to have a family.

Bob: I'd had three children in my first marriage and my first wife's influence on my kids was so enormous that they are children I still don't know terribly well. Because of Julie, my relationship with our two young sons is totally different. My closeness to our children comes from my closeness to Julie — it is a natural extension of our relationship. She is very wise and very demanding. She's very good for me. She shares her problems with me, but she doesn't expect me to solve them. This is the first relationship in my life where I don't feel like I always have to fix something.

Julie: After ten years, people still don't see us as a married couple, and sometimes refer to me as his daughter.

Bob: Because of our age difference, I'm probably more aware of my own mortality than Julie is of hers; but how wonderful to have a life that you want to hold on to for as long as possible. I've just started a new business, which at 64 is totally ridiculous, but I want to have on my tombstone, "He lived while he was still alive."

"I just wanted to be with her at all costs."

DAVID & REGINA PORTNOY

SHE STAYS HOME AND CARES FOR THEIR THREE PRE-SCHOOL CHILDREN, WHILE HE WORKS TO SUPPORT THE FAMILY FINANCIALLY. FOR DAVID AND REGINA, THE COMMITMENT OF THEIR MARRIAGE VOWS ALLOWS THEM TO SEE THIS PERIOD AS A STAGE IN THEIR LIVES, ONE WHICH HAS ITS OWN REWARDS TO BALANCE THE HARDSHIPS.

Regina: *I came from a family of ten kids, stairsteps one after another. I always wanted a large family myself because that was what I was used to. It never occurred to me that I wouldn't be able to stay home and raise my own children. My own mother was always there for us. She was always my role model.*

David: I see Regina's family and I want the same thing for my kids. Although finances are sometimes a struggle for us, I can't see her away from the kids. I see us as an endangered species. Almost everyone I know…both parents work and they only have one or two kids.

Regina: *Every year my own parents really make a big deal of our wedding anniversary. The longer we're married and the more kids we have, the more I appreciate the accomplishment of staying married. Right now our life is so centered around the children that we practically have to make an appointment to have a conversation.*

David: It's hard to hold hands when you are holding the kids.

Regina: *Even though I came from a large family, I had no idea how much time being a mother would take from being a wife.*

David: Becoming a father threw me for a loop. I had no idea…their infancy was especially hard on me. All the crying, diapers, and lack of sleep was something I wasn't prepared for.

Regina: *If your marriage can survive colic, it can survive anything.*

David: Our third child was born prematurely and was critically ill. Regina is Catholic and I'm Jewish, so I wasn't raised praying in the same way she was; but seeing my little son so helpless in the hospital, I learned how. For the first time I realized the power of prayer.

Regina: *Our youngest is scheduled for his third surgery next month. It seems like it's hard to get out of debt. I wasn't prepared for the financial responsibility of having kids. Not that it isn't worth it, but it is hard.*

"I see us as an endangered species. Almost everyone I know…both parents work and they only have one or two kids."

DAVID & KATHY ROSETTI

FOR DAVID AND KATHY ROSETTI, MARRIAGE PROVIDES A PRIVATE STRUCTURE FOR THE RAISING OF CHILDREN. IT ALSO BRINGS AN INCREASED SENSE OF RESPONSIBILITY FOR THE WORLD WHICH THEIR CHILDREN WILL INHERIT.

David: We had only gone out for a short time when I started thinking about marriage. The whole community was behind us getting together. We were the only single teachers at the school.

Kathy: I applied for the teaching job there because the little town had the same name as my grandfather. It was a good thing we liked each other because there were no other eligible men around.

David: Sometimes I want to argue and then just leave it. She wants to talk about everything in such depth. In the middle of the night I hear a big sigh and I think "Oh oh, here we go again...."

Kathy: Maybe. Sometimes I do seem like a nag, but for me communication is crucial. I don't want to talk to him, but with him.

David: Sometimes I think it's best just to leave things alone.

Kathy: It seems like most women feel responsible to keep the conversation lively. I am not comfortable with long silences. After I've been alone in the house with the babies all day, I'm looking forward to adult conversation.

David: ...I need to switch gears and have some time to unwind before I get too engrossed with things at home. I can hear my father's voice coming out of my own mouth saying, "just let it go." We don't walk on eggs around here. We're not afraid to argue. When she makes a mountain out of a molehill, I call it a "Westchester crisis."

Kathy: He accuses my mom of the same behavior. At least he doesn't talk behind our backs.

David: I wonder how she can do the 24 hour, seven day a week job with such good cheer. I've learned a lot about patience and love by watching her with our children. I'm a much more empathic school principal now.

Kathy: Being a mother certainly makes me much more empathic towards people in general. I look at everyone as somebody's baby. Issues seem more urgent when you are a parent.

David: I can't just say "not in my backyard" anymore because I realize the next generation is counting on us.

"I can't just say 'Not in my backyard'
anymore, because I realize the next
generation is counting on us."

MAGGIE MOON & TAYLOR RICKARD

THEY EXCHANGED VOWS AND WEDDING RINGS TWO YEARS AGO AFTER SEVERAL YEARS IN A COMMITTED RELATIONSHIP.

Maggie: I was the "other woman" for the first six weeks of our relationship. I knew she was it for me and I loved her on any terms. If she stayed with her girlfriend, I would still be her friend. It wasn't about possession — I just wanted her in my life, preferably as a lover, but I would accept as a friend.

Taylor: That sort of unconditional love was very powerful and, ultimately, very seductive. I'd been married to a man for 14 years and his biggest weakness was providing emotional support. Maggie's nurturing empathy and unconditional constancy felt really good by comparison, though it was scary as hell. I wasn't looking for love. If anything, I was running from it.

Maggie: For me, it is the person, not the package. If Taylor was a man, I'd still fall in love with her.

Taylor: Neither one of us are man-haters. There are good people of both sexes. Maggie and I are good for each other.

Maggie: We have complementary strengths and weaknesses. So, the whole is greater than the sum of the two. There is no competition between us because we have two different spheres of influence.

Taylor: My husband was very competitive with me and we couldn't give each other the support we both needed.

Maggie: Taylor is absolutely smarter and more educated than me, but I'm much more intuitive and instinctive. If people are too similar, they can't help but compete.

Taylor: Our relationship is not built on living up to others' expectations for us. I am my own harshest judge. Being raised a Southern lady, I was born into a set of expectations that just don't fit. I actually like the person I am a lot better than the person I'm supposed to be!

Maggie: I was expected to be a Christian Science healer like my mother. Now, my expectations are also my inclinations, so I have surrendered to who I am and find great comfort in my relationship with Taylor.

Taylor: We have both been through some rough stuff to get comfortable with ourselves. We both have a sense of who we are as individuals and who we are together. Her approach to things is a lot different than mine. We generally end up in the same place, but we get there from incredibly different perspectives.

Maggie: It comes down to accepting. I know her glitches, and I love her, glitches and all. She is perfect for me. She's not a perfect human being, but she is perfect for me.

"I'd been married to a man for 14 years and his biggest weakness was providing emotional support."

CHAPTER 3

"When you get married, there is no way to know what's in store. God protects us from that knowledge. It would be too much to bear."

Mark Whittle & Mary Catherine Ellwein

MARRIED ONLY SEVEN MONTHS AT THE TIME OF THIS PORTRAIT AND INTERVIEW, MARY CATHERINE IS UNDERGOING CHEMOTHERAPY FOR HER THIRD EPISODE OF CANCER. THIS TIME IT IS CONSIDERED INOPERABLE.

Mark: When I proposed to Mary Catherine, I decided to play life through the heart instead of through the mind.

Mary Catherine: It was a deliciously emotional, full, moment when I said "yes." I knew my cancer pushed in his face the biggest risk of loving someone. We struggled for years with this and when he proposed, we just gave it up.

Mark: My internal struggle whether we should get married or not set a tone in our relationship for years. My life now is our life and that is for me the biggest difference between being married and living together.

Mary Catherine: Our married life together has been totally centered around my illness. The day we left for our honeymoon, six weeks after we were married, I started having symptoms that hinted that my cancer was reoccurring.

Mark: We tried to pretend like it was just a little weird incident, but deep inside I was very disturbed. My newfound courage was being tested much earlier than I expected.

Mary Catherine: You try to prepare yourself for the worst, but of course you never really can. When it became apparent that the cancer had spread so much it was inoperable, I felt really angry. At the same time, Mark and I were experiencing these close, very conscious, real days and nights together that were some of the most blissful times in my life. We were getting bad news right and left, but somehow something between us kept us stable. We were experiencing the pain and the fear at the same time as this incredible closeness.

Mark: It does seem that when her illness gets dire, it brings out parts of my nature that are really surprising to me. I had never thought of myself as a particularly nurturing person, but that seems to be what is needed now and I seem to be able to be there for her. The big things, like our careers, seem trivial and the small things, like tucking a blanket, seem important.

Mary Catherine: He has surpassed all expectations and been so wonderful through all of this. He surprises me, impresses me, and doesn't let me down. I think there is a part of me that can't admit how hard this must be for him, because it's almost unbearable to acknowledge. There's a huge amount of guilt that I convinced Mark that I was worth the risk because I was in remission. Every day, every month, every year that we have is realized as a gift. We don't have the luxury to deny things, put things off. There is a sense of immediacy in everything we do. It is as if the cancer intensifies time.

Mark: Our marriage has opened me up to one whole arena of the emotional world. Mary Catherine provides a mirror and sounding board for my own feelings. Instead of backing away from strong emotions, I experience them as they happen and am able to live my life more fully. I feel like she's opened my shell. As a scientist, I always lived the life of the mind, searching for answers and explanations. Loving Mary Catherine has taught me to simply experience and accept my emotions.

*"When I proposed to Mary Catherine
I decided to play life through the heart
instead of through the mind."*

MEDGAR & CAROL GAGE

DESPITE HER FEARS AND MISGIVINGS, AT THE TIME OF THIS PORTRAIT AND INTERVIEW, CAROL HAD TAKEN MEDGAR BACK IN AN ATTEMPT TO KEEP THEIR MARRIAGE TOGETHER.

Carol: After our oldest son was born I felt like we should get married; either that or call it off.

Medgar: I didn't feel ready, but my mother advised me it was the right thing to do.

Carol: He wanted to be with me without the commitment.

Medgar: I felt trapped.

Carol: He can't stand not doing what he wants when he wants it. Part of growing up is learning to be unselfish.

Medgar: My father left us when I was four and I never really knew what it was like for a man to be a husband and father. It's a terrible feeling growing up without a father. I see my sons watching me, copying me. I never, never want to do to my boys what was done to me. I think Carol knows she's got me for that reason.

Carol: He says he's got to be around for the kids, but I need someone around for me.

Medgar: I can't figure out what Carol wants, but I have to believe that one day I'll get it right.

Carol: A little bit of consideration would be nice. If I cry and get upset, it seems like he gets angry instead of comforting.

Medgar: I feel like she is blaming me for something when I don't even know what I did.

Carol: If he cares, it seems like he would want to find out what I'm feeling. It's like he gets defensive and mad when I'm feeling unhappy.

Medgar: I do feel responsible for Carol's feelings, just like I do for the kids.

Carol: He gets to the point where he acts like he just doesn't care....

Medgar: That's because I get so frustrated, I don't know what to do. When I served time in jail for beating her, I knew I had to learn to control my temper or I'd lose my family and then I'd be lost.

Carol: After he got out of jail, my mother really didn't want me to take him back. But we have a family here and somehow have got to learn to get along.

"When I served time in jail for beating her, I knew I had to control my temper or I'd lose my family and then I'd be lost."

John & Sharon Holohan

In addition to the everyday challenges of raising two young daughters, John and Sharon Holohan also deal with their older son's multiple handicaps from cerebral palsy.

John: *Although none of our three kids were from planned pregnancies, once we settled down to the surprise, we just accepted it and carried on from there. When our son was born so prematurely, it never occurred to us that he wouldn't be okay. The first time the doctors told us he'd never be a basketball player, we didn't realize the extent of his disabilities.*

Sharon: Having a handicapped child takes up as much physical and emotional energy as five healthy children.

John: *When she got pregnant again, we were both plenty anxious.*

Sharon: Every time John brought up his fear, I didn't want to talk about it — as if somehow the words could make our fears come true.

John: *We had every prenatal test available, but we swept our feelings about the outcome under the rug. When we got married, we didn't have a care in the world.*

Sharon: His physical therapy and constant care are a full time job, even if he didn't have two younger sisters.

John: *The expenses on one paycheck can get pretty tight, but we've done all right for ourselves. We struggle, we get behind on our bills, but somehow we always bail ourselves out.*

Sharon: Our patience is challenged by our kids, especially our son's handicap. You can't rush when a child is in a wheelchair.

John: *Our sense of humor has become very developed over the years. There's a lot of teasing and joking in the family. You'd go crazy if you took everything too seriously.*

Sharon: It would be nice if just the two of us could get away, but it just isn't possible. Right now we just enjoy talking and thinking about it.

John: *The glue that holds us together is that we love each other — we have since we met 16 years ago. Having the children might cause us to run out of money and have too much responsibility to travel, but it's still just the two of us in our bedroom when the children are asleep.*

Sharon: If anything, our sex life is better now since I know I can't get pregnant.

John: *At least that's one thing we don't need to worry about since she got her tubes tied.*

"When we got married, we didn't have a care in the world."

BOB & JOANNA ECKSTROM

WHEN THEY GOT MARRIED 20 YEARS AGO, THEY ASSUMED THEY WOULD HAVE CHILDREN. FOR MOST OF THOSE YEARS THEY HAVE TRIED UNSUCCESSFULLY TO CONCEIVE. NINE YEARS AFTER THIS PORTRAIT AND INTERVIEW, THEY REMAIN CHILDLESS.

Bob: *The last time we tried* in vitro *fertilization we implanted five viable eggs and felt certain we had a good chance at pregnancy.*

Joanna: I said it would be the last try, but now we are embarking on another attempt. I am not ready to stop yet....

Bob: *And I am, because I have seen her get her heart broken again and again. Over and over she climbs the stairs of hope and there is no walking back down. You crash onto the floor, hard. It's hard for a man to understand what a woman feels like. The desire for having a baby is much stronger in her than it is in me.*

Joanna: Since we know it is practically impossible for me to get pregnant now without medical assistance, it's freed up our sex life and we can be together without thermometers and anxiety.

Bob: *Having sex on demand is not great for intimacy. We would track her fertility to the hour. It was crazy, but I never felt it was tearing us apart. I think Joanna is very brave. I cannot always understand her drive to be a mother, but this struggle has probably strengthened us as a couple. Marriage is two people sharing a vision. In our case, it has been an obsession.*

Joanna: There are times I get angry that Bob doesn't feel the same way I do. I surprise myself. I never knew I was so stubborn. It is something I just have to go with. I am the only one who's going to know when I've had enough.

Bob: *I can try to tell her. After as many attempts as we have made, the odds are incredibly low. We are going to try yet again, one more time to conceive. I want to protect us both from disappointment. God knows we've tried....*

Joanna: I am not through trying quite yet. It's hard to think about adoption when you're trying to have your husband's baby.

Bob: *And I'm not sure I'm ready to go under the scrutiny of an adoption agency. I'm not ready to settle for something. And if we do adopt a child, I don't want to do it with that attitude. Adoption is not simply the other side of the coin. It is much more complicated than that. Our procreative urges are complicated. I am much more committed to having my own child than taking in someone else's.*

Joanna: Doing that would be admitting defeat. It is important to me to have Bob's child. The whole thing with family, carrying on names. It's something you almost take for granted until you can't have it.

"It's important for me to have Bob's child.... It's something you almost take for granted until you can't have it."

Mark Solomon & Peggy Eliott

Several years after his marriage to Peggy, Mark sold his business and re-embraced his religion of Orthodox Judaism.

Peggy: After 12 years I can finally say I'm glad I'm married to Mark. We've had a very tumultuous marriage. After five years of courtship, I was 38 when we finally got married. The dream to have a child, a home — all the trappings that go with marriage — was probably as important to me as the fact that I loved Mark. I wanted to be just like my brother and sister.

Mark: ...and just like my ex-wife!

Peggy: I wanted all the things his ex-wife had.

Mark: Just as I was getting rid of all that stuff, she was coming and wanted it all again.

Peggy: We bought a place, I had a baby, but there was tremendous tension and struggle along the way. I am Mark's third wife and each of us brought a lot of emotional baggage to the marriage.

Mark: I first got married when I was a teenager and it's a completely different relationship than entering a marriage in your late 30s. Five or six years ago I completely changed my life. I sold a family business and re-embraced my religion. The real difference in our relationship now is that I've broken out of old habits that I carried with me through the first two marriages and into the first half of this one that were making me miserable. How can you be happy with someone if you are not happy with yourself? I'd spent years struggling with the behavior of my partner before I realized that change has to come from within. It's not so much what happens around you as how you react to it.

Peggy: When he sold his business, I realized how important Mark's money was to me. He was my chance to live the life I had always imagined and wanted.

Mark: I made a lot of money, but I didn't think of myself as successful because I hated my work. It's almost as if the person she fell in love with was the person I was trying to outgrow and leave behind.

Peggy: We couldn't even talk about his lifestyle changes for a year. I was so furious.... I felt tricked, betrayed.

Mark: So did I. I was struggling to survive and she wasn't able to give me any support.

Peggy: I came to realize that even with these external and internal changes going on, the man I loved was still intact. The intelligence and generosity didn't go away. I used to really resent his observance of Shabbat on Friday night, but now I even participate because I'm really glad we are together. This is where I want to be.

"We couldn't even talk about his lifestyle changes for a year. I was so furious.... I felt tricked, betrayed."

ERNIE & MARIAN SHERGOLD

MARRIED 22 YEARS, ERNIE AND MARIAN SHERGOLD WERE DEVASTATED WHEN DOCTORS IN THEIR NATIVE ENGLAND DIAGNOSED THEIR SON CRAIG AS HAVING AN INOPERABLE, AND PROBABLY FATAL, BRAIN TUMOR. A RICH AMERICAN BUSINESSMAN HEARD ABOUT THE SITUATION AND ARRANGED FOR CRAIG TO BE BROUGHT TO THE UNITED STATES WHERE AN EXPERT SURGEON DISCOVERED A VERY RARE, BUT OPERABLE, CONDITION. CRAIG IS PICTURED HERE WITH MARIAN AND ERNIE SHORTLY AFTER THE SURGERY WHICH SUCCESSFULLY REMOVED THE TUMOR.

Marian: When you get married, there's no way to know what's in store. God protects us from that knowledge. It would be too much to bear.

Ernie: A good sense of humor and free flowin' tears help you get through.

Marian: Believe me, we have had our fights, but our love for our kids binds us together. My oldest was 12 years old when Craig was born. What a blessing — did we have a party!

Ernie: When Craig was diagnosed with a brain tumor, it was like being in physical pain.

Marian: Craig was hurting so bad, it took our breath away. Ernie just denied it at first. When the hospital offered us a cup of tea, I knew it was bad news. We had just lost my mom and the thought of losing our baby boy was unbearable. I just wanted to wrap him in a blanket and then run away.

Ernie: You feel so helpless. You want to take care of your child, but you are just pushed aside when your child is in the hospital.

Marian: Our life came to a halt and we spent all of our time at the hospital. The worst hell you can imagine is to have your child deathly ill and in pain.

Ernie: Some couples fall apart, but we just held onto each other and cried. We've never been closer than during his operations.

Marian: Not that there haven't been times when the pressure got so bad, I just wanted to run away. I tell you one thing, the worry of losing your child puts everything else in perspective.

Ernie: I always respected Marian's judgment and intuition about Craig. Moms know their kids better than the doctors. I always followed her lead.

"When you get married, there is no way to know what's in store. God protects us from that knowledge. It would be too much to bear."

CARLOS & SANDY MEJIAS

CARLOS AND SANDY MEJIAS HAVE HAD A VERY CLOSE RELATIONSHIP WITH HER PARENTS OVER THE YEARS. HAVING HELPED SANDY AND CARLOS ESTABLISH THEMSELVES IN BUSINESS AND RAISE THEIR YOUNG CHILDREN, HER PARENTS NOW FIND THEMSELVES IN NEED OF HELP. AT THE TIME OF THIS PHOTOGRAPH AND INTERVIEW, SANDY'S FATHER WAS SUFFERING FROM TERMINAL CANCER AND HER MOTHER WAS BED-RIDDEN WITH DEGENERATIVE ARTHRITIS.

Sandy: If there was a tally right now, I would definitely still owe the debt to my parents. They helped us financially and emotionally every step of the way.

Carlos: I would do it all over again, even if I knew now how much care Sandy's parents would need when they got older, because it's been wonderful for our children to grow up with their grandparents. I don't even know my grandparents' names. I don't think of them as in-laws. Sandy's father is a real role model for me. I have tremendous respect for him.

Sandy: Our marriage is quite different than a childless couple. My parents and children really cement the bond.

Carlos: Marriage is like a marathon. It's a big challenge, but if you succeed, there's great satisfaction.

Sandy: I feel a real spiritual aspect to the institution. I am definitely not meant to be alone. I truly feel like Carlos is my other half. If you're lucky enough to find your other half and procreate, I think there's tremendous meaning there.

Carlos: I grew up without a father and I know how that feels. I feel that the children really suffer without both parents and the world wouldn't get very far without children.

Sandy: I think life would be harder for me if I were alone in the world. It feels good to be needed and to have someone to talk with. Carlos has characteristics that are lacking in me that I really admire.

Carlos: I could say the same thing about Sandy. Our dream is one day to go back to the life we shared when we first met, working the dog shows and training.

Sandy: Our youngest will be 18 in ten years and maybe then we'll have time to be together. We've lost a baby, are raising a child with cerebral palsy and another with learning disabilities, and my elderly parents need care around the clock. Any one of these things can tear a marriage apart.

Carlos: Or make it stronger. You don't want to teach your children to be quitters. You have to focus on your goals and endure.

Sandy: Watching my parents age makes me see how fast times goes by. It makes me realize that we're all just passing through. It helps me through the hard parts to realize everything is temporary. Our marriage is one thing that can endure.

"If there was a tally right now, I would definitely still owe the debt to my parents."

MARTIN RUBENSTEIN & MARTIN SCHWARTZ

SOMETIMES A MARRIAGE CAN SURVIVE SEEMINGLY INSURMOUNTABLE OBSTACLES. OTHER TIMES THE PROBLEM RUNS SO DEEP THAT THE MARRIAGE MUST END. MARTIN RUBENSTEIN'S AND MARTIN SCHWARTZ'S FIRST MARRIAGES COULD NOT STAND UP TO THE POWER OF THEIR TRUE SEXUAL ORIENTATION.

Martin S: For seven years we struggled to keep our marriages together, but ultimately the force of our attraction was too strong for us to be apart.

Martin R: I am 19 years younger than Marty. When I met him, my wife and I were expecting our first child. He had older children and had been married for some time. Our relationship with each other was always totally honest, whereas our relationships with our wives and family were filled with secrets.

Martin S: Eventually we felt like we were committing adultery when we slept with our wives.

Martin R: Now my first child is 25 and Martin is an important part of her life. We are very close to our children. When they were young, they introduced me as their father and Martin as their stepfather.

Martin S: My children were a lot older and had a much harder time dealing with our relationship. If I were born today, I probably would never have married. I knew I had a different sexual orientation, but I thought it was just experimentation.

Martin R: We are not naive. We know that there is still a lot of homophobia in this world, but that's their problem, not ours. We accept who we are and accept others as they are.

Martin S: We both wear wedding rings and are a committed couple. Our bands are fashioned from one length of gold.

Martin R: We're very different in many ways, but it's as if one completes the other.

Martin S: We don't have separate bank accounts. We own everything together, even our clothes.

Martin R: Like any relationship, whether between the same sexes or different sexes, there is a division of labor.

Martin S: I do the cooking, he washes the dishes.

Martin R: I do the bills, he does the gardening.

Martin S: It's like having an extra pair of hands.

"Eventually we felt like we were committing adultery when we slept with our wives."

ARTHUR & LINDA STEIN

THE MARRIAGE COMMITMENT DOESN'T INFLUENCE JUST THE RAISING OF YOUR OWN CHILDREN. ARTHUR AND LINDA STEIN WERE BOTH DIVORCED WITH TEENAGE CHILDREN WHEN THEY MARRIED. TOGETHER, THEY FOUNDED AND NOW RUN A CHILDREN'S WISH FOUNDATION, WORKING WITH TERMINALLY ILL CHILDREN TO GRANT THEIR REQUESTS.

Arthur: At 43 I had a heart attack that made me really question the way I was living my life. My work and my marriage were both up for question and I decided to make a change...that life was too short for such compromises.

Linda: The death of my daughter put my first marriage under irreparable strain because my first husband and I had such different styles of grieving. We spent all of our energy trying to keep her alive and when she died, everything fell apart. I began to question the meaning and importance of everything. I had always felt that my needs were the last on the list, after my husband and children were taken care of. I started to think about what I wanted and I realized I had to change a great deal about my life.

Arthur: Linda and I had known each other professionally, over the telephone, for quite some time. And, we got divorced within a month of each other.

Linda: After being married to a doctor, who was never there for me emotionally, I'm luxuriating in Arthur's empathy. For the first time in my adult life, I feel like my feelings are allowed.

Arthur: My first wife was much more interested in maintaining her lifestyle than any satisfaction I got from my work. Linda and I are both committed to helping others, especially each other.

Linda: The struggle with my daughter's illness, and the divorce following, forced me to take charge of my life for the first time. Marriage this time around is a totally different situation. Of course, second marriages have a whole new set of problems. I still can't get my mother to take my first wedding picture off the wall. She's disappointed that she can no longer say, "My son-in-law, the doctor."

"My work and my marriage were both open to question and I decided to make a change...that life was too short for such compromises."

NORMAN & DELORES GOINS

NORMAN AND DELORES ARE RAISING THREE NIECES ALONG WITH FOUR CHILDREN OF THEIR OWN. MONEY PROBLEMS WERE A CONSTANT SOURCE OF FRICTION BETWEEN THEM UNTIL NORMAN HAD A SEVERE HEART ATTACK, THREE MONTHS BEFORE THIS PORTRAIT AND INTERVIEW.

Delores: The night before Norman had his heart attack we had a terrible argument over something so stupid I've honestly forgotten what it was about. We went to bed without saying "good night" to each other. I woke up in the night and was still angry. When he told me "good morning," I never even opened my mouth. When it was time to go to work, I just walked through the door without saying a word and he was just standing there looking at me. I slammed the door as hard as I could, got in the car and drove away. At work at the hospital, someone told me to go to the emergency room, that my husband was down there. When I saw that big man laid out flat with all those tubes running through him I thought "Oh God, what have I done?" I thought I would go mad if I couldn't apologize to him and tell him I love him. The idea that I would never have a chance to make it right cut me in two. I prayed like I have never prayed before and I made a vow right then and there that I'd never go to bed mad or leave my house angry again.

Norman: The Lord has a way of teaching us what we need to learn. I feel grateful to have a second chance — to appreciate my life — the responsibility as well as the satisfaction of my family. I didn't want to leave Delores behind with these seven kids. We all depend on each other. Children need a mother and a father.

Delores: My boys would especially be lost without their father. They look up to him in every way — they don't copy the mother, they copy the father. I started thinking how my children are obedient, respectful kids and how many of their decent values come from their father. I had to almost lose him to appreciate this. Daily life has so many little irritations it's easy to lose sight of the main thing — that we love and respect each other. Silly stuff doesn't matter anymore.

Norman: For some reason it seems like people can't learn things without suffering. It makes you a better person.

Delores: It took a heart attack for us to stop taking each other for granted.

"For some reason it seems like people can't learn things without suffering."

CHAPTER 4

"...the monolith that is us."

JIM ROBINSON & CORNELIA JOHNSON

JIM AND CORNELIA UNDERSTOOD THAT AN INTERRACIAL MARRIAGE MIGHT BRING PROBLEMS. IN THE BEGINNING, THEY MET THEIR SHARE OF OPPOSITION, ESPECIALLY FROM HIS FAMILY.

Jim: We knew that our families would have a hard time accepting us as a couple. Interracial marriages, especially here in the South, are still unusual. We lived together for a couple of years before we got married, and got along so beautifully. We had to do the right thing for us and let the rest of the world make up its own mind. I suppose my own mother would have disowned me if she had been alive.

Cornelia: My in-laws said they didn't want "that nigger" in their house and to this day he has relatives I've never met. But an individual can change things easier than laws and over the years his parents have come to know me and grown to love me.

Jim: I was in Central High School in Arkansas when the 101st Airborne was sent in to guard us against eight black children bused in by the new desegregation laws. When integration was forced on us in 1955, I saw that people were basically the same, it's only the unknown that was frightening. I taught elementary school later on and got rid of any racism I had grown up with. I learned a lot about our common humanity in the classroom.

Cornelia: We often see people nudging and pointing when they see us together. We even have an expression. I'll say, "Honey, we're on TV again."

Jim: She has so many goals and ambitions. If she wants to hit the campaign trail and run for office, I'll be right beside her. I like to laze around and watch TV when I am not at work, but Cornelia never sits down.

Cornelia: Maybe I can be like Ed Robb and go from being a police officer to the [Virginia State] Senate! When we were first married it seemed like Jim changed for a while, like he thought now that he's my husband, he has to make all the decisions. We had to go through some difficult adjustments, but we have both learned to not make major decisions without consulting the other. I'm not afraid to get into an argument, but Jim might clam up if I come on too strong. Jim seems comfortable with what he has achieved, but I'd like to live in the governor's mansion.

Jim: She pushes herself so hard, I worry about her not taking care of herself. She is always on the go, doing things for other people, myself included, so I don't feel neglected; but I worry about her health and well being. Everything she does, she does well. She is the most caring person I've ever known.

Cornelia: The constant stability of his support keeps me on track. He's always there for me. It is as if his belief in me helps me believe in myself. I know my drive and ambition makes me hard to live with, so I really appreciate his patience.

"We had to do the right thing for us and let the rest of the world make up its own mind."

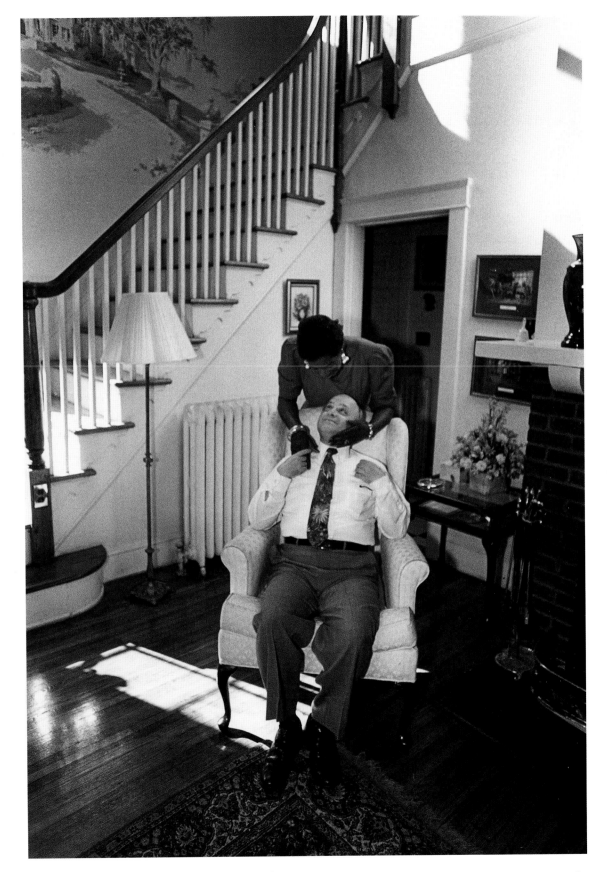

Philip Murray & Roma Starczewska-Murray

Both Philip and Roma were divorced when they met while working for the Voice of America. Married for 13 years at the time of this portrait and interview, they describe the adjustments necessary between them when they married.

Philip: I think I was somewhat of a martinet at the beginning of our relationship. I was used to being a drill sergeant; it was the way I had raised my four kids on my own.

Roma: I wasn't very appreciative of being treated like a child; but the more I learned about his past and got to know him, the more I could understand his behavior and we could work things out. I survived Poland, so I could survive Philip's irrational behavior.

Philip: She went through both the German and Russian occupation. I still have a short fuse, but I've mellowed as I have gotten older.

Roma: Thank God! It was difficult for him to say, "I'm sorry"....

Philip: ...and it was difficult for her to accept my apology. I used to hate it when she gave me the silent treatment.

Roma: Over the years he's come to accept that life is often difficult, but that is no reason to lose your temper.

Philip: Sometimes it's a little difficult for us when Roma is my director at the radio station.

Roma: He has a problem taking directions from a woman. I can accept that; yet I won't back down if I feel I am right and he's wrong. It's probably a strength in our relationship that we are both in the same business because we can understand the pressures.

Philip: We're both extremely opinionated and stubborn, which can be a problem when we disagree. But, we are also extremely compatible because we are so much alike.

Roma: We have our craft shows, our gardening. We like the same people, books, movies.

Philip: St. Francis is very special to us. We were both raised Catholic, and even though we're not regular churchgoers....

Roma: ...I feel like we practice our own private religion.

"We were both raised Catholic and even though we're not regular churchgoers...."

"...I feel like we practice our own private religion."

NATHAN & DORIS YODER

THE YODERS WERE BOTH RAISED IN THE MENNONITE RELIGION WHICH EMPHASIZES A PLAIN, GODLY LIFE AND DISCOURAGES CONTACT WITH THE OUTSIDE WORLD.

Doris: Being a housewife is a proud calling for a Mennonite woman. We each have our own autonomous household, but we get together for a sewing circle or berry picking. I was not raised to be career minded. I always expected to be a mother in the home.

Nathan: Children are a fulfillment for women.

Doris: A woman who does not marry and have a family must always wonder.

Nathan: The highest priority of our marriage is to serve God. To us, this life is just the rehearsal for the big event, the day when we will be in heaven. Not that we are disinterested in things here on this earth, but we don't count that next pleasure as if this life is all that matters. That gives us a perspective of patience that can be a great strength in marriage. Ours is a living faith, not just something we bring out on Sunday morning.

Doris: My husband has the ultimate say-so in decision making, as the head of the family.

Nathan: No organization functions well without a leader.

Doris: I look at his responsibility towards me as a source of protection. It causes me no frustration, in fact it gives me comfort.

Nathan: So many people see submission as a negative thing. We don't perceive a husband's leadership role as anything but man's obligation. It is totally unfair for a wife to submit to a husband unless he in turn submits to God. This is an important aspect of leadership.

Doris: When our daughters are about three, they wear the white cap, which symbolizes our respect for the Lord and our husband.

Nathan: Tradition has both good and bad implications. I suppose it could mean a rut, but the good side is that it is a very stabilizing factor. You don't have to spend all your time making up rules; you can get on with the details of living. We avoid TV and movies because they affect our thoughts, which in turn affect our lifestyle, which affects our eternal destiny. As a result, we take our thoughts very seriously.

"It is totally unfair for a wife to submit to a husband unless he in turn submits to God."

AL & MARINA OLIVERA

AL AND MARINA OLIVERA HAVE BEEN MARRIED FOR MORE THAN 20 YEARS. CHILDLESS BY CHOICE, THEY LAVISH ATTENTION ON EACH OTHER AND THEIR DOG, HIGGINS.

Al: *We decided we wouldn't have kids before we were even married.*

Marina: I went through a period when I thought maybe we were making a mistake. We took care of a friend's two year old for a while and I realized we had made the right decision. I honestly don't want to take on that responsibility. I can really see how children can snuff the romance in a relationship.

Al: *Our choice for childlessness almost provokes some people.*

Marina: Especially those who have been staying awake night after night for years with small children.

Al: *Life gets so busy, even without children, that we have to make a recommitment to spend time together. There's no such thing as "happy ever after." It's an on-going project. We get away together every 90 days for a week or ten days. We love to travel and spend time together.*

Marina: We sometimes feel a little envy from our friends with kids because we can do so much together. We love having something to look forward to. Even that date on Saturday night keeps us going through the week. When Al gave me my engagement ring, he said, "Marry me and I'll make you a queen." My friends at work called me Queenie. My mother tells Al that I was not at all spoiled when I left her house, and he ruined me! But I am delighted, right Al! (She nudges him.)

Al: *Yes, dear. (They both laugh hysterically.) Seriously, though, marriage is too often put aside for work and family. I think husband and wife should be the first priority for each other.*

Marina: Self-esteem is such a big issue. We live in a culture where everyone fears vanity.

Al: *But you can't love someone else more than you love yourself. Feeling good about yourself is a prerequisite for feeling good for others. I get great joy from making my wife happy.*

90

"*Our choice for childlessness almost provokes some people.*"

Jimmy & Brucie Parnell

Jimmy and Brucie grew up as "beach kids" in the 1950s and '60s. They found that the life they wanted (centered around surfing and the beach) often clashed with the values of their parents. Despite some economic hardships, they have built their marriage and family around this way of life. The children surf competitively and the family spends weekends traveling to surfing contests. Jimmy is often a judge and occasionally still a competitor.

Jimmy: Both of our parents have been married going on 50 years. Our marriage had been traditional until Brucie went back to work. I help around the house more than I used to, but she still has two jobs.

Brucie: I have a hard time letting go of responsibilities around the house. I would rather do something myself, because then I know it will get done right. Jimmy probably could and would do more around the house if I would let him do things his way as opposed to my way.

Jimmy: The differences in the way Brucie and I were raised come back to haunt us rearing our own children. Brucie tends to be more corrective on a daily basis and I'm the big gun for bigger problems.

Brucie: I can't imagine raising teenage boys alone. I lean on his support constantly.

Jimmy: I was in the first generation of surfers. It had a reputation as a rebel sport and my own parents weren't very supportive. They sent me to a military school to try and get me away from it. I have always been behind my kids' love of the sport. I've given them the support I missed.

Brucie: Surfing puts the whole family where we like to be — on the beach. We both love to watch the kids compete.

Jimmy: Unfortunately you can't live your children's mistakes for them. Everyone has to learn for themselves. We really enjoyed an extended adolescence until our mid-20s. Maybe that will protect us from flipping out and having a mid-life crisis.

Brucie: We know a lot of kids 18 to 25, and I think they look at us as role models.

Jimmy: The institution of marriage is in such a shattered state that young people are really looking for something to believe in.

Brucie: Sometimes when Jimmy is down in the dumps, I feel really drawn to him and want to build him up. We've had some hard times financially, but this has drawn us closer together. I derive strength from the commitment of "for richer or poorer." Now that I have a job, I think Jimmy appreciates all the more the things that I was doing at home.

"Surfing puts the whole family where we like to be — on the beach."

Tom & Ruth Klippstein

Tom and Ruth have lived on a commune (they call it an "intentional community") for most of their 24 years together. This physical, emotional, and financial proximity with others doesn't seem to have hindered their intimacy.

Ruth: We feel so tight, so close to each other, that sharing our lives with others in a communal situation is not a threat to our relationship. Our nuclear family has remained intact within the group, but this lifestyle gives us access to other emotional and financial resources. It relieves us of the pressure of trying to be all things at all times for each other.

Tom: Living in a group like this lets me have close women friends, as well as other men friends. We both spend most of our time here at Springtree, so we do not have access to office mates for friendship. One thing that makes our marriage unique is that we have spent the last 15 years working together everyday.

Ruth: The original intention of the group was to keep hands on one's life as much as possible. Home schooling the children, raising and growing our own food, building our own shelter.

Tom: There have been about 25 children reared here in the community. Most are now college age or older, so it is quite a different place. The long hallway in the main house used to reverberate with the thundering of small feet.

Ruth: It was really good for our son to have other children around. Sometimes we think our lives would be simpler if we lived alone now, but then we think it would not necessarily be as fulfilling. We have very few trappings in our life; we've never even discussed owning a house. We like to be free to travel because it gives the opportunity to invent each day.

Tom: We've been so important to each other, to the exclusion of other things, that I think sometimes our son has suffered because of the monolith that is us. He always believed that neither one would take his side, that we would always stick together. Every time he wanted something or did something wrong, I think he might have felt a bit overwhelmed by the strength of our relationship.

"...the monolith that is us."

PETER SHERAS & PHYLLIS KOCH-SHERAS

THEY MET DURING THEIR INTERNSHIP IN PSYCHOLOGY, AFTER PHYLLIS WAS RECENTLY DIVORCED. BOTH ARE CLINICAL PSYCHOLOGISTS, WITH A SPECIALTY IN MARRIAGE COUNSELLING AND SEX THERAPY. AT THE TIME OF THIS PORTRAIT AND INTERVIEW, THEY WERE WORKING ON A BOOK ABOUT CREATING SUCCESSFUL COUPLES.

Phyllis: Marriage was really unfashionable in the 1970s and I'd just gotten out of a failed marriage. I remember asking him "why did you have to come along now, just when I was starting to be independent?" I was determined never to feel under someone's thumb again. Perhaps the fact that Peter was a bit younger helped me assert myself. My first husband was older than me and I was much more compliant when I was younger. The first time I got married, it was such a huge step. I was a virgin on our wedding night.

Peter: For us, we had our careers, we bought a house and lived together for quite a while. What was really nice was when we got married, nothing really changed, because the commitment was really there.

Phyllis: At the beginning, I was defiantly assertive....

Peter: ...and I was much more passive, but over the years we seemed to have met in the middle somewhere. I'm still the calm one and Phyllis is the emotional one, but the differences have mellowed as we've grown older together.

Phyllis: At first we were philosophically committed to total equality in all things between us. But through the years we have come to realize that the burden of responsibilities in running a family and a career constantly shifts, and from time to time one or the other of us has to carry a heavier load. Over time, it balances out.

Peter: If we ever break up, it won't be about our feelings. We are not our feelings — they change like the weather. What doesn't change is the commitment to work things out. We get along much better now that I've learned not to hold myself responsible for her feelings. Love is not a thing; it is a declaration, a possibility.

Phyllis: My commitment is to continue to build on this life that I love, that we have made together. We've been through times when our life together was pretty unsatisfying, but we never hid from our problems and through counselling I learned to look at my own responsibility for what was happening to us.

Peter: It is not that we never feel like giving up, it's just that we don't — even when things feel hopeless.

Phyllis: That is probably what commitment is.

Peter: Our prescription for a troubled relationship is "take two actions, and call me in the morning." In couple coaching, we coach each other on who we want to be. We declare our intentions and hold each other accountable....

Phyllis: ...and that makes the relationship alive, with possibility for growth and change.

"We are not our feelings. They change like
the weather. What doesn't change is
our commitment to work things out."

ROGER & DIANE ABRAMSON

MARRIED IN 1954, THEY AND THEIR FOUR CHILDREN HAVE THRIVED WITHIN THE LIFESTYLE OF THE MUSIC INDUSTRY. UNCONVENTIONAL AND NON-JUDGMENTAL, THEY HAVE AN UNUSUALLY CLOSE-KNIT FAMILY BOND.

Roger: When we got married in the '50s, men and women had very clear roles and expectations for each other. We were no exception and our relationship changed and grew through the social upheaval of the '60s and '70s, and adjusted to the Reagan years as well.

Diane: A couple, a family, is always connected and influenced by the world around them. Like most women of my generation, I got married at 19. Now that would be considered extremely young, but back then it wasn't at all unusual.

Roger: Our cluelessness was almost beyond comprehension. Love led to marriage and we never questioned it.

Diane: Nine months later I had a baby. Then another one, then another one. Life just kind of unfolded and we just followed along. Our kids question and consider everything. It's like we had less options. I think we didn't have such high expectations for our marriage as people do now. If you question everything and are always wanting what you don't have — no wonder there is so much divorce.

Roger: Loyalty, friendship, and respect are a lot more important than money or sex.

Diane: I've seen a lot of friends breakup over unrealistic expectations about money and sex.

Roger: I'm a spender and Diane is a saver — maybe our sex life keeps us together! Who knows — it's a mystery that we don't really explore.

Diane: Roger would probably love to talk about the meaning of life — the "whys" and "so forths," but I tend to live moment to moment. I don't tend to look back or plan for the future.

Roger: Diane is wonderfully straightforward and matter-of-fact. She makes being married very comfortable and easy for me. Her companionship is the most vital part of my life. It gives me a sense of connectedness, as opposed to being adrift.

Diane: There were plenty of times when we didn't get along, but our commitment to each other helped us work things out — either by changing or sometimes just ignoring the problem.

Roger: I am willing to just forget about it. Neither one of us has to win every argument. It's not worth the wear and tear. I would probably be more successful in the music industry if I had a less easygoing personality, but I'm not sure Diane and I would be any better off. Young people are always searching for the ultimate, both personally and professionally; but when you get older you realize that life isn't about ultimates, but a continuing process of little pieces that create the whole picture.

*"When you
get older
you realize
that life
isn't about
ultimates, but
a continuing
process of
little pieces
that create
the whole
picture."*

Ludwig & Beatrice Kuttner

LUDWIG IS A BUSINESSMAN AND BEATRICE AN ARTIST.

Ludwig: She always surprises me. I love it that I can't predict. I am always working on letting go of preconceived ideas. We are both becoming more like ourselves as we grow older.

Beatrice: It takes years to trust being yourself. No one is so secure that they never second guess. To do something to please another is one thing, but to be something else other than who you are is ultimately doomed to failure. One day the whole relationship will fall apart.

Ludwig: It's harder for me to talk about things, but I know it's the only way to grow together. It is scary for me to share my dislikes or insecurities, but Trixie has always accepted my feelings.

Beatrice: It doesn't threaten me at all. On the contrary, it lightens my load to know exactly how he is feeling.

Ludwig: It's a lot of work and effort to do something well. Marriage is no different. All relationships reach stages where you can dig deeper or break apart.

Beatrice: We never try to change or improve each other, only ourselves.

Ludwig: The strange thing is, for couples to get closer, each one has to do what they really want to do, not what they think the other one wants them to do. You teach each other by example, but you cannot force change on another. That has to come from within. She has taught me so much about appreciating beauty, just by the way she lives her life. I enjoy the money I make so much more because of her artistic eye.

Beatrice: I think the most important thing is to be open to change. If you get stuck on one level of consciousness, it's very life-denying. One definition of life is change. We cannot hold onto old ideas, we have to go forward.

Ludwig: Sharing your heart is an act of courage, especially if you had an emotionally deprived childhood. It took me many years to feel safe enough to share my thoughts and fears. Trixie's love sets me free.

Beatrice: Loving Wiggie has been a very healing process for me with my own father. I have let go of anger. He took his own life. I now realize it was out of frustration at not being able to communicate. If we let ourselves get stuck, and we don't grow and change, life can become unbearable.

"To do something to please another is one thing, but to be something else other than who you are is ultimately doomed to failure."

H. & Katy Ball

H. and Katy reminisce about the early years of their marriage. Having successfully managed some difficult times, they also speculate about a future challenge — that of growing old together.

H: *I remember seeing her tenderness early in our relationship. The way she treated animals was a signal of what was inside, but the hardest part of our marriage was early, when Katy really was not happy with herself. I didn't know what was going on. We lived together happily, then as soon as we got married, she seemed miserable.*

Katy: I had a lot of anger towards myself and I reacted by withdrawing from H.

H: *It hit me hard when she wanted to be alone our first Christmas together. I remember trudging through the snow to the cabin where she was staying and wondering whether the person I married was still there.*

Katy: He gave me the space I needed to work things out and was smart enough to not blame himself for my unhappiness. The thing that keeps us together is our mutual support and, if there are weaknesses, it is through support that they are shed. If H. had not given me loving support as I went through such a difficult personal crisis of self-doubt when we were first married, we might not be here together today.

H: *I had a lot to learn. In the beginning I saw some of Katy's immaturities as embarrassing to me personally, like they were my fault. I'm glad I no longer see her as someone to be judged.*

Katy: I love to see H. grow in his role of father. I think it is incredibly manly to be a husband and father. Even though those roles aren't held up in popular culture, women do find them appealing.

H: *I find it appealing to think of two people growing old together and still being bright-eyed with affection for one another.*

Katy: When I ask him if he'll still love me when I am old and grey, he doesn't answer.

H: *Well, I don't want to encourage it, but I'm not afraid of it. Of course, I haven't faced any physical limitation of old age yet, so it is all pretty theoretical. No one knows what's going to happen tomorrow, but it seems like it would be easier to grow old together rather than alone.*

"No one knows what's going to happen tomorrow,
but it seems like it would be easier to
grow old together rather than alone."

CHAPTER 5

"We might not always be perfect,
but the ideals are always
there to aspire to."

VAUGHN & PAT KALIAN

THEIR MARRIAGE OF 20 YEARS ENDED IN DIVORCE OVER A BETRAYAL OF THE HEART. FIVE YEARS LATER THEY FOUND THAT FORGIVENESS IS POSSIBLE. THEY HAD BEEN REMARRIED FOR SIX MONTHS AT THE TIME OF THIS PORTRAIT AND INTERVIEW.

Pat: I don't think we could have broken out of our old patterns of behavior that stopped working for us as we approached middle age if we hadn't had those years apart. When I was younger, it was harder for me to admit my mistakes and it took until now for me to realize I'm not responsible for Vaughn's happiness or anger. We were so young when we became a couple, neither one of us could appreciate the other. We no longer take each other for granted. We have a renewed sense of trust since we betrayed each other and let each other down. We had to earn it the second time around and, since it has been tested, we have a deep appreciation for its value.

Vaughn: Pat understands the stress my work places on me since she's been out in the world working. The weight of my responsibilities is more real to her now. I used to put all my energy in my work and let Patty steer our domestic life, but now I make an effort, too.

Pat: You need to understand yourself to have intimacy with another. If you marry young like we did, it's harder to separate your actions from your reactions. It's easy to lose yourself in your role of wife and mother, or husband and father. Mid-life crisis is a time when you allow yourself the time to meet individual needs that need to be addressed. Every individual has to face a reckoning, a fundamental assessment of where do I, or we, go from here.

Vaughn: The synergistic affect of external stresses causes something to break. In my case, I left my job and my marriage broke up at the same time. Now, I have work I am even more excited about, and our relationship is better since our remarriage; so, I can't really say I have regrets for problems in the past.

Pat: We wouldn't have the good things we have going for us without the previous stresses, which at the time, certainly seemed disastrous.

*"We have a
renewed sense of
trust since we
betrayed each
other and let
each other down.
We had to earn
it the second time
around and, since
it has been tested,
we have a deep
appreciation for
its value."*

CRAIG & PHOEBE WOOLLEY

MANY MARRIAGES HAVE BEEN DESTROYED BY ALCOHOLISM, BUT A SURPRISING NUMBER HAVE ALSO BEEN DESTROYED BY THE ADJUSTMENTS REQUIRED BY SOBRIETY. MARRIED FOR MORE THAN 50 YEARS, CRAIG AND PHOEBE WOOLLEY RECOUNT HIS TREATMENT FOR ALCOHOLISM AFTER 30 YEARS OF MARRIAGE.

Craig: Alcoholism is a disease of denial. For at least ten years I kept the problem like a guilty secret in the back of my mind. Your family and work get less and less as booze becomes more important. Over the years, Phoebe had gotten good at covering my tracks, but my company stepped in and put me in an intensive rehabilitation program.

Phoebe: When they asked me how bad his drinking was at home, I said he had recently lost three overcoats.

Craig: I was the breadwinner so her reaction was to protect me from the company's inquiry. She could have said a lot worse! I felt humiliated and relieved when I told her I was being committed to an alcoholic treatment center. She looked at me and said, "It's about time." The only way to recover is to start speaking the unmitigated truth. It was a start.

Phoebe: I had a huge reservoir of anger built up over his erratic, unreliable behavior over the years — which I had denied as much as Craig denied his drinking. Thankfully, Craig's treatment involved me and I was able to confront the miserable times his drinking had inflicted on our family.

Craig: When we left treatment, there was nothing left unsaid and 20 years later we're still able to be more honest with ourselves and each other. It gives you great confidence to be free from manipulation and denial.

Phoebe: It didn't happen overnight, but the treatment program gave us the tools to communicate honestly and build a future together that has been good for both of us. I had to change as much as Craig did. Everything I had done to be a supportive wife was actually enabling dishonesty. Change is hard, but necessary and always worth the effort.

Craig: She lost her halo, but we became a lot closer, more like equal partners instead of the derelict husband and long suffering wife. We became more like the young people we were when we fell in love the first time. I no longer can blame my faults on booze.

Phoebe: And neither can I. We can no longer use his drinking as an excuse for any problems between us. It's just us, with no place to hide.

"We can no longer use his drinking as
an excuse for any problems between us."

BILL & JILL RINEHEART

BILL AND JILL WERE MARRIED IN 1940 AND HAD A "TRADITIONAL MARRIAGE" IN WHICH BILL SUPPORTED THE FAMILY FINANCIALLY AND JILL RAISED THE CHILDREN. AFTER THE CHILDREN WERE GROWN, SHE WENT BACK TO COLLEGE AND GOT HER OWN APARTMENT. DIVORCE SEEMED LIKELY, BUT INSTEAD THEY RECONCILED AND THE PROPOSED DIVORCE SETTLEMENT WAS TURNED INTO A MARITAL CONTRACT WHICH THEY HAVE LIVED BY FOR MORE THAN TEN YEARS.

Jill: When our oldest child was a baby, we had an argument and he simply wouldn't listen to me. He said, "you're not supposed to think, you are supposed to do what I say." I was so furious and frustrated that I packed my trunk, picked up the baby and took the train to my mother's. But, I had to go back to him because there was no way I could support myself with a child. I began to realize that money equaled independence.

Bill: My behavior towards her that she found unacceptable wasn't a lack of respect, as much as simply behaving in a way I thought a man was supposed to behave. In my family, the man always took care of the woman. We never thought of financial independence.

Jill: He didn't have to, he always had it. His grandmother didn't have a checking account. I felt like he said "no" to everything I wanted to do. It was never my turn. It was always his turn. I could no longer live in such a patriarchal world. I had never been economically independent and it was something I really needed. I always looked like I was rich, but I never had a damn dime of my own. After I graduated from college, I secretly rented my own apartment.

Bill: She really wanted to be independent. It was like we were dating again. We didn't take each other for granted.

Jill: I loved that little apartment. I loved my independence. After a few years we negotiated a marriage contract, which evolved from the economic settlement we were drawing up for a divorce. It gave me some capital so I could be economically independent. I knew Bill and I could never be completely emotionally independent from each other... not after 40 years of marriage.

Bill: My lawyer was very upset, he said everything was going her way....

Jill: I said to "tell your lawyer that for 40 years everything has gone your way. Now it's my turn." I wanted more than room and board and use of the family car. If we had gotten divorced, I would have gotten a financial settlement.

Bill: So we figured why don't you just take the settlement and we'll stay married. I had a lot more appreciation for everything she did around the house after she was gone for two years. I have spent all my life with Jill. She's not replaceable. I always wanted to work things out. I can't imagine being without her.

Jill: We get along so well now. We have been through so much. We've thrown all the old myths away and live in reality. We have had to struggle and fight, really hurt each other, to get to the place where we are now. We're something stronger than our own individuality. We are a couple, a family and part of our community.

"We have had to struggle and fight, really hurt each other, to get to the place where we are now. We're something stronger than our own individuality."

ROBERT & EVELENA MICHIE

MARRIED FOR 33 YEARS, ROBERT AND EVELENA MICHIE HAVE BOTH WORKED SEVERAL JOBS OUTSIDE THE HOME AND RAISED SIX CHILDREN. REVEREND MICHIE RUNS HIS BAPTIST MINISTRY WITH HIS WIFE BY HIS SIDE.

Robert: One of the duties I really enjoy in my ministry is counseling couples to prepare them for their wedding vows. We do not believe in divorce, so it is not something to take lightly or unadvisedly. I could never be an effective minister if I were not a married man. I cannot imagine my ministry without my wife at my side. I can draw from my own experiences when I talk to young people about marriage.

Evelena: Marriage should be a partnership.

Robert: I think divorce is the worst thing happening in society today. It does terrible things to the children. Besides our faith, being able to talk to one another is the most important thing in a marriage. If you don't like runny eggs, you've got to speak up; you don't want to spend 33 years eating something that you do not like.

Evelena: Sometimes you've got to just say, "I am sorry."

Robert: I think it is especially hard for men to apologize, but it's really important to not let your pride get in the way of the truth. The funny thing is, it really makes you feel better about yourself if you openly admit your mistakes.

Evelena: You shouldn't be afraid to speak the truth to each other. Really, it is the only way to keep things going. I feel like I can say anything I want to my husband.

Robert: I cannot see that a lot of secrets can do anyone any good. A man and a woman united are a great deal stronger than standing alone. We share the housework alongside with our feelings. When our children were young, if I got home before she did, I would think nothing about putting a pot on the stove or making the bed — it was always easy for me to get a mop and clean the floor because she was helping me (bring in money to the household).

Evelena: I am helping him and he is helping me. That's the way it's always been. We taught our kids to pitch in, too. Everyone carries their own weight in this family.

*"It's really important not to let
your pride get in the way of the truth."*

Tien & Rose Fang

THEY MET BRIEFLY IN 1943 IN CHINA. THEIR COURTSHIP CONSISTED OF SIX YEARS OF LETTERS WHILE MR. FANG WAS AN OFFICER IN THE CHINESE MILITARY STATIONED IN WASHINGTON, D.C. WHEN THE COMMUNISTS TOOK OVER SHANGHAI, HE PROPOSED THAT SHE COME TO AMERICA TO BE HIS BRIDE. SPEAKING NO ENGLISH, SHE IMMIGRATED TO THE UNITED STATES AND WAS MRS. FANG WITHIN A WEEK.

Tien: The marriage in the West is like a pot of hot water on the boil that can too quickly turn to steam and disappear. A Chinese marriage is a pot of cold water on a slow flame that gets warmer and warmer over a lifetime.

Rose: Patience is a word we are very comfortable with.

Tien: Rose is not only my wife, I see her as my sister and my best friend, as well. Many times I will yield to her, I don't have to win every disagreement.

Rose: The Chinese wife knows her duties. She has respect for her husband and expects his respect in return.

Tien: It was much harder for me to know how to be a good American style father. Rose and I have Chinese expectations, but our son and daughter are Americans. I was in the restaurant business for 30 years and wouldn't get home until after the children were in bed. They would be in school in the daytime, there was never time to be close. Maybe if I could have spent more time with them I could have talked to them more about how to be a husband and a wife, and they would not get divorced.

Rose: My English was not so good and the children didn't speak Chinese. We wanted them to be Americans and they wanted turkey, not duck, on the dinner table. Like most Americans, they were always in a big hurry and didn't have much time to listen.

Tien: If pride comes in to a marriage relationship, it is the beginning of the end. It takes humility to really consider what your partner is saying, what they need — that is what we mean when we talk about patience and respect.

Rose: There is no doubt that my husband understands me and I know him better than anyone. The language of our heart is Chinese. I now realize we should have spoken Chinese to our children, but we wanted them to speak good English because we wanted them to do well in this country.

Tien: We were wrong, even with the best intentions.

Rose: My husband is a generous man, but I would never ask for anything that was too hard to get. He always wanted to buy me a mink jacket, but I don't really want it.

Tien: Contentment is happiness, not wanting things. There is no contentment in that. These are beliefs I wish I had shared with my children. We sent them to college and graduate school, but these are not things you learn in school. We spent a fortune sending them to 16 years of higher education, but I wish we had taught them Chinese.

"A Chinese marriage is a pot of cold water on a slow flame that gets warmer and warmer over a lifetime."

FREDERICK & PHYLLIS SPEAR

A RETIRED PROFESSOR OF FRENCH, HE ENJOYS GARDENING WITH HIS WIFE. THEY BOTH LOVE TO TRAVEL AND ARE STILL CLOSE TO THEIR TWO GROWN CHILDREN.

Frederick: Every Memorial Day, Phyllis and her identical twin sister would march in the parade in Methuen and they always caught my eye.

Phyllis: Growing up as an identical twin, I have never known what it's like to be alone. My sister and I were very, very close. I had to make a new identity for myself when I got married.

Frederick: I never felt like an intruder on that relationship. Her twinness was never a problem for me. I always got along well with her sister. Being an only child, my own mother was sometimes more of a problem between us. The main challenge for us was the same as for all married couples — communication. Perhaps we had a bit more of a challenge because of the silent communication she had with her twin for years. Even today, she sometimes expects me to divine things.

Phyllis: Women are more intuitive, anyway.

Frederick: One of the greatest things to come out of the feminist movement is that men are learning to talk about how they feel, as well as how they think. This really makes true intimacy more of a possibility.

Phyllis: We are really enjoying coming and going as we please since the children are grown and Frederick is retired. It is not uncommon to see older couples who have been together for a long time start to look alike. The years together give you similar reactions.

"It's not uncommon to see older couples who have been together for a long time start to look alike. The years together give you similar reactions."

DAN & LORENE ROBINSON

MARRIED FOR MORE THAN 50 YEARS AT THE TIME OF THEIR PORTRAIT AND INTERVIEW, THEY TALK ABOUT THE DIFFICULTIES OF OLD AGE WITH THE SAME PRAGMATISM AND HUMOR THAT THEY BROUGHT TO ALL OF LIFE'S CHALLENGES. SEVERAL MONTHS LATER, THEY WERE PARTED BY DEATH.

Dan: The first time I met Lorene, she was the nurse anesthesiologist when I had an appendectomy. After the operation, they only had a bed on the obstetric ward. As soon as I was coming to, the first thing I saw was this pretty nurse holding a baby. She says "we thought you had appendicitis but this is what we found!"

Lorene: I had seen Dan before, at his sister's, and thought he was cute. All the nurses thought it was so funny that we had to put him on the maternity ward.

Dan: She said I was too thin and she wanted to fatten me up, so I moved across the street from the hospital. I don't know who was keeping an eye on who!

Lorene: Dan was always on the road during the early years of our marriage and it seems like I had to raise our children mostly on my own. Having two in one year made it impossible for me to make my own money. He worked hard to provide for us, but it was hard to make much back then.

Dan: People had to amuse themselves. There wasn't much entertainment, like TV or the movies. There was not much divorce, either, because people had to talk to each other — there wasn't anything else to do!

Lorene: It seems like the time is just gone.

Dan: I don't know where it has gone, but is surprises you to realize that most of it is behind you. I feel like life is closing in on us, like we're running out of time. It seems like I can't catch up from day-to-day. I get so impatient and nervous. When I went to run an errand today, the whole afternoon just slipped by....

Lorene: ...and I forgot he had gone and I didn't know where he was. That made me feel panicky, like I was lost in my own home.

Dan: She gets awfully frightened if she doesn't know where I am. She is deaf in one ear and her eyesight is not the best. When I leave the room she starts calling out "where are you?"

Lorene: I've had right many strokes. I feel confused.

Dan: Sometimes I feel like she is trying to take advantage of me. Seems like I can't walk down the hall without her calling after me. You've got to roll with the punches, I suppose. I've had to learn to talk slowly and be patient.

"I feel like life is closing in on us, like we're running out of time."

BUSTER & DOROTHY WILLIAMS

MARRIED MORE THAN 60 YEARS, THEY ARE NOW SEMI-RETIRED. SHE RUNS THE BORN AGAIN HOLINESS PENTECOSTAL CHURCH ON SUNDAYS. THEY ALSO HELP CARE FOR THEIR GRANDCHILDREN, SIX OF WHOM WERE LIVING WITH THEM AT THE TIME OF THIS PORTRAIT AND INTERVIEW.

Dorothy: I must tell you that life is hard. If I did not have Jesus on my side, I don't think I could have made it. The answer in marriage is, one or the other of you has to know Jesus. You do not run to your mother or daddy when you have a problem; you don't run to drugs or alcohol to get backbone, you run to the Lord. I reared my children that way. Seems like parents nowadays don't teach their children right from wrong.

Buster: Looks like children run wild now. They all take that old dope stuff. Young men nowadays just don't understand that you have got to work to keep things going. Nothing comes easy, and it seems like they want everything to be easy. We both worked hard all of our lives, but we are still going strong.

Dorothy: There were times in my life when I had to be washing clothes at 12:00 or 1:00 at night and be up and out on the job at 7:30 in the morning. That was what was needed to be done.

Buster: I used to get up at 3:00 a.m. to work on the horse drawn milk truck, but that didn't bother me. I knew we were both doing our fair share; both of us have given 100% of ourselves.

Dorothy: The reason so many women are alone today is because they left God out of the plan. He teaches you to do the right thing. Then some men leave no matter what you do....

Buster: You can drive your man away if you ask too much of him. A man cannot carry a woman on his back.

"I must tell you that life is hard."

KEMPER & MATTIE THOMPSON

KEMPER WAS SIX YEARS OLD WHEN MATTIE WAS BORN. HE TOLD HER MOTHER THAT ONE DAY HER LITTLE BABY WOULD BE HIS WIFE. HE'D WALK MILES TO HER HOUSE EVERY SUNDAY, AND 15 YEARS LATER, IN 1929, HE KEPT HIS PROMISE. THEY CELEBRATED THEIR HONEYMOON WITH A 28-CENT PIECE OF CANDY.

Kemper: Farm work is never steady. I was always going from job to job....

Mattie: ...but he could always find work.

Kemper: I took up carpentry by myself and built our house. Since I retired, I spend a lot of time fixing up the house.

Mattie: Seems like I can hardly get my work done with him underfoot all day. (Laughter from both.)

Kemper: Trouble with knowing how to be everything from a plumber to a blacksmith to a mechanic is everyone always needs a little piece of your time. I quit school in third grade, but I've always been able to take care of my family.

Mattie: I was ten years old when I started school because it was too far to walk when I was younger. I quit at 15 to get married. I had to skip one day a week to stay home and do the wash. Back then we had to haul our water, chop wood, feed the chickens, and milk the cow. I thought life would be a little easier when I got married, but I just hopped out of the frying pan into the fire. (She pats Kemper's hand.) I had seven children in ten years. When my oldest was 12 years old I worked in the orchard as well as running the house. We grew our own vegetables and raised our own meat, but we still always needed money.

Kemper: God has been good to us, we never lost a child. As hard as she had to work, everyone of them was healthy.

Mattie: Now we have 18 grandchildren and nine great grandchildren. I loved it when our own children were little. I could put them to bed and know where they were. I don't know where they are now. I used to love that feeling of having them tucked safely in bed.

Kemper: They are gray-headed now and Mattie still worries over them.

Mattie: I sit back now and wonder how we raised all those children and worked from dawn to dusk. But you do what you have to do, I reckon.

Kemper: Seems like medical bills keep us jumping nowadays.

Mattie: I've never had anything handed to me on a silver platter, but Kemper has always worked hard right beside me. Our kids and grandkids have all kinds of stuff nowadays, but they aren't any happier than we were. I don't like all this living together like they do now. It's too easy to run away and you don't really get nowhere.

"God has been good to us, we never lost a child…. They are gray-headed now and Mattie still worries about them."

Magruder & Posy Dent

Mac and Posy met on a blind date shortly after Mac came back from the Pacific after World War II. They were married within eight months.

Posy: We went into our marriage vows with a lot of awe.

Magruder: An oath is a promise to God. When I made a vow to Posy, it was also a promise to God. To say marriage is "just a piece of paper" is like saying "it's just a written contract." I wouldn't want to go into business with someone who had that attitude!

Posy: There's nothing casual about the marriage contract. It gives you something to think about — something to refer to and remind yourself of as life goes on. We might not always be perfect, but the ideals are always there to aspire to.

Magruder: The legal and sacred obligations of a married couple affects the whole organization of society. A community is a group of families and a family is the source of each individual.

Posy: When a marriage breaks apart through divorce it affects more than just that family. It ultimately affects the entire community.

Magruder: When we got married we had a sense of these obligations, not only to ourselves but to the community.

Posy: When you've made a lifetime commitment to someone, forgiveness is an important part of the plan.

Magruder: Every day I forgive her (they both start to laugh) for what she does, or what she says....

Posy: ...or what I don't do! I say I'm sorry a lot — even when I'm right! (They both laugh again.) But seriously, how can anyone know that they can get along with someone for the rest of their life? For me it was a matter of trust. I'd never met anyone I trusted more than Magruder and I still feel that way about him today. His integrity made me feel safe. Not because he's always perfect, but because I know he has a clear sense of right and wrong.

"We might not always be perfect, but the ideals are always there to aspire to."

HOW I MEET THE PEOPLE I PHOTOGRAPH

CHAPTER 1

LINDLEY & YUKARI FRAHM (1993)
My husband met Lindley at a biotechnology conference in Philadelphia. Lindley and Yukari live in California.

RODNEY & TAMMY HARDING (1992)
She is the great granddaughter of the woman who taught me how to garden in 1972, and the sister of James Riddle.

BILL CAMPBELL & MARYANNE VOLLERS (1991)
Bill is a distant relative/close friend and Maryanne has become one of my best friends.

KURT & TAMARA TOTTEN (1993)
They hired me to photograph their wedding in 1993.

KIP & LENI SORENSON (1990)
Kip is a carpenter who built my darkroom and office.

SAT BIR & SIRI KRISHNA KHALSA (1993)
They are my husband's yoga teachers.

JAMES & ANDREA RIDDLE (1990)
James is Tammy Harding's brother. James and Andrea separated several years after the photograph was made.

RALPH & MARY MORONEY (1990)
Mary was my brother's neighbor, then one of my photography students.

MERT & JUDY MARTIN (1993)
Mert is a cabinetmaker and Judy is Maryanne Vollers' sister. They met while Mert, who was working for H. Ball, was helping build Bill and Maryanne's "dream house."

MATTHEW & AMY PAPPERT (1990)
Matthew is the former boyfriend of the daughter of Rose and Tien Fang and a friend from my New York City days.

CHAPTER 2

PAUL & ROSEMARY SUMMERS (1990)
Rosemary, my brother's wife's sister, was first married to my second cousin once removed.

DAVID & NEILA SMITH (1992)
Neila was my husband's co-worker.

GARY & CANDI VESSEL (1991)
I photographed Gary and Candi in Seattle, Washington, for a *Glamour* magazine story about moms who stay home with the kids.

RONALD & ZARINA (ANN) GORDON (1992)
They are friends of a friend.

JOHN & DIANE LEGGE (1993)
Diane works for Sandy and Carlos Mejias' dog training school in Alexandria, Virginia.

BARCLAY & AGGIE RIVES (1990)
Barclay is one of the "kids I grew up with," and Aggie is a friend.

BOB & JULIE GOTTSCHALK (1993)
Friends of friends, they have since separated.

DAVID & REGINA PORTNOY (1991)
I photographed them in St. Louis, Missouri, for the *Glamour* magazine assignment.

DAVID & KATHY ROSETTI (1991)
I photographed them in upstate New York for the *Glamour* magazine assignment.

MAGGIE MOON & TAYLOR RICKARD (1993)
They are friends of my photography associate of 19 years, Kathy Bowers.

CHAPTER 3

MARK WHITTLE & MARY CATHERINE ELLWEIN (1993)
They are friends of a friend.

MEDGAR & CAROL GAGE (1993)
I met Carol in a shelter for battered women while working with Maryanne Vollers on an as-yet-unpublished magazine article.

JOHN & SHARON HOLOHAN (1993)
Their son is in physical therapy in Northern Virginia with my niece, the daughter of Sandy and Carlos Mejias.

BOB & JOANNA ECKSTROM (1990)
Joanna is my husband's first cousin. She is also first cousin to Marina Olivera and Sandy Mejias.

MARK SOLOMON & PEGGY ELIOTT (1992)
Peggy was my teaching assistant at the International Center of Photography in New York.

ERNIE & MARIAN SHERGOLD (1991)
I met them while on a *People* magazine assignment.

CARLOS & SANDY MEJIAS (1991)
My college roommate (now my sister-in-law), she is first cousin to Joanna Eckstrom and Marina Olivera. Sandy's father, "the General," died several months after this photograph was made. Her mother died five years later.

MARTIN RUBENSTEIN & MARTIN SCHWARTZ (1991)
They are friends of a woman in my last book, *Home of the Brave*.

ARTHUR & LINDA STEIN (1991)
I met them on a *People* magazine assignment about a children's wish foundation in Atlanta, Georgia.

NORMAN & DELORES GOINS (1993)
They are sometime employees and long-time friends.

CHAPTER 4
JIM ROBINSON & CORNELIA JOHNSON (1993)
Cornelia is a well-known and popular policewoman in Charlottesville, Virginia.

PHILIP MURRAY & ROMA STARCZEWSKA-MURRAY (1993)
They now own the house my husband lived in when he was in grade school.

NATHAN & DORIS YODER (1990)
They are friends from a *People* magazine photo-essay about a wonderful school for the mentally retarded.

AL & MARINA OLIVERA (1990)
She is first cousin to Sandy Mejias and Joanna Eckstrom. Al and Marina live in New Hampshire.

JIMMY & BRUCIE PARNELL (1991)
I grew up with Brucie and Jimmy in Virginia Beach, Virginia.

TOM & RUTH KLIPPSTEIN (1990)
They are friends of friends.

PETER SHERAS & PHYLLIS KOCH-SHERAS (1992)
They are friends of friends.

ROGER & DIANE ABRAMSON (1983)
They were next door neighbors in New York City.

LUDWIG & BEATRICE KUTTNER (1988)
Our sons were together at Saint Anne's School and we became friends.

H. & KATY BALL (1990)
They were in my book *Giving Birth* 15 years ago. H. was the contractor for our new house and for Bill Campbell and Maryanne Vollers' house.

CHAPTER 5
VAUGHN & PAT KALIAN (1993)
I met Pat during a "spouse's activities" session at a biotechnology conference in Florida.

CRAIG & PHOEBE WOOLLEY (1993)
Parents of my long-time friend and associate, Kathy Bowers, they live in California.

BILL & JILL RINEHEART (1992)
I went to Saint Anne's School (class of '69) with their daughter in Charlottesville.

ROBERT & EVELENA MICHIE (1990)
They are pillars of the community in Charlottesville.

TIEN & ROSE FANG (1992)
They are parents of a close friend and former photography student, Wei Li Fang.

FREDERICK & PHYLLIS SPEAR (1990)
I saw them gardening in their yard when I was on vacation in New Hampshire and asked them if they would be in a book about marriage.

DAN & LORENE ROBINSON (1990)
We bought our farm from them in 1987 after we moved back to Charlottesville from New York City. Lorene died three years after this interview.

BUSTER & DOROTHY WILLIAMS (1990)
They are Delores Goins' parents.

KEMPER & MATTIE THOMPSON (1981)
They are former neighbors of Rose and Tien Fang's daughter, Wei Li.

MAGRUDER & POSY DENT (1993)
My closest friends from my parents' generation, Posy and Mac have been a model for me in my own marriage. Mac died a few months after this picture was made, but years later his words still inspire me.

ACKNOWLEDGMENTS

This project was many years in the making, and I would never have made it to the finish without the unwavering support of my husband, David. He has been my guiding light.

It takes more than one champion to get a book in print, and Brooks Johnson, curator of photography at The Chrysler Museum of Art, is definitely the godfather of this work. There were difficult times when he singlehandedly kept the project going. It is also my good fortune that his wife, Germaine Clair, believed in the work and agreed to grace its pages with her strong sense of design.

Funding for this book and exhibition was provided by generous grants from the Adrian & Jessie Archbold Charitable Trust, the Camp Foundation and the J. L. Camp Foundation. I extend my deepest thanks to Arthur Mahon, Sol Rawls and Jamie Camp. I'd also like to thank Anthony Hirschel of the Bayly Museum, Alison Devine Nordström of the Southeast Museum of Photography, Ronald Crusan of Waterworks Visual Arts Center, and Elizabeth L. Francis and Wanda A. Marks of Rawls Museum Arts. These directors agreed to co-publish *With This Ring* with The Chrysler Museum of Art, and their support made this book a reality. My parents, Bruce and Caroline Sherman, gave me both emotional and financial support. Their name is synonymous with generosity.

I would also like to thank the entire Chrysler Museum staff for the roles they played in mounting the exhibition. Most especially, I want to thank Georgia Young, curatorial assistant, for her invaluable help on this book.

Of course, the people to whom I'm most indebted are the couples on these pages, for there would be no book without their cooperation. Their generosity of spirit was a privilege to experience.